TAHITI TRAVEL GUIDE 2023

French Polynesia island; The ultimate travel
pocket guide for First-Timers to Explore
the culture and traditions.
Hidden Gems: lesser known beaches, and
everything you need to know.

By

Douglas.K.Wilson

All rights reserved. No part of this publication may be reproduced, distributed, or transmitted in any form or by any means, including photocopying, recording, or other electronic or mechanical methods, without the prior written permission of the publisher, except in the case of brief quotations embodied in critical reviews and certain other noncommercial uses permitted by copyright law.

Copyright © (Douglas.k.wilson), (2023).

TABLE OF CONTENTS

The MAGICAL PARADISE OF TAHITI
TAHITI DAILY LIVING ROUTINE
CULTURAL VARIETY AND HISTORY
CULTURAL DIVERSITY
GEOGRAPHICAL LOCATION

CHAPTER 1: WELCOME TO TAHITI
TAHITI's CAPITAL CITY
REGIONS IN TAHITI
RELIGIONS IN TAHITI
TAHITI's SURROUNDING ISLANDS

CHAPTER 2: THE NATURAL BEAUTY OF TAHITI

CHAPTER 3: MAKING TRAVEL
SEASON TO VISIT
TRAVEL AND ENTRY REQUIREMENTS
USEFUL TRAVEL ADVICE
BUDGETING A TRIP TO TAHITI

CHAPTER 4; HEALTH INFORMATION.
Tahiti's medical centers
Tahitian Health System
ADVICE ON TRAVELING HEALTH
EMERGENCY CONTACTS AND RESOURCES

CHAPTER 5: GETTING AROUND TAHITI
IN TAHITI, TRANSPORTATION
Tahiti's Traffic Laws And Advice
Tahiti bus routes and bus fares
Taxi Services and Costs in Tahiti
Popular Routes for Motorcycling and Cycling in Tahiti
Popular Routes for Motorcycling and Cycling in Tahiti

CHAPTER 6: OPTIONS FOR ACCOMMODATIONS IN TAHITI
Tahiti vacation spots
ELEGANT HOTELS
RESORT
CLAMPING
OVERWATER BUNGALOW
Rentals for holidays
Tahiti accommodation websites and how to utilize them

CHAPTER 7: TOP TOURIST ATTRACTIONS IN EACH CITIES IN HAITI AND THE COUNTRY'S FESTIVALS.
Days Trips in Tahiti

CHAPTER 8: FOOD AND RESTAURANTS.
Tahiti's regional specialties
Tahiti's traditional cuisine.
Tahiti's Seafood Prices And Variety
TAHITI RESTAURANT WEBSITE

CHAPTER 9: LANGUAGE AND CURRENCY
USEFUL TAHITIAN PHRASE TO KNOW
The System of Tahitian Money

CHAPTER 10: CLUBS AND NIGHTLIFE IN TAHITI
Live Music Locations
Cultural and traditional performances
Restaurant and Food Suggestions

CHAPTER 11: BEACHES AND MUSEUMS IN TAHIT.
Hidden Gems: Lesser-known Beaches in Tahiti
Tahiti's water sports and beach activities

CHAPTER 12: TIPS FOR A MEMORABLE TAHITIAN VACATION
Snorkeling and Scuba Diving

Yachting and Sailboarding
Aquaplaning and Jet Skiing
Visits with Dolphins and Whale Watching
Adventures Off-Road on the Island

CONCLUSION

The MAGICAL PARADISE OF TAHITI

"Tahiti is a location where reality vanishes into an entirely magical world. Its emerald-green mountains, sapphire lakes, and balmy wind create a paradise right out of a fairy tail "

Once upon a time, a tropical paradise known as Tahiti was located in the middle of the huge Pacific Ocean. All who ventured to this enchanting island's shores were enchanted by its emerald-green mountains, azure lagoons, and immaculate white sand beaches.

According to legend, Tahiti was constructed by the gods themselves with their heavenly hands, who sprinkled it with their love and turned it into a paradise of amazing beauty.

Dreams might fly there, the soul could find refuge, and the spirit of adventure may flourish.

The cultural legacy of Tahiti is quite rich. The warmth of the islanders' hospitality embraced the lively Polynesian culture, which reverberated throughout the atmosphere.

Visitors were warmly welcomed to explore the enchanting traditions of the Tahitians, who are renowned for their generosity and close connection to nature.

Life on the island developed in a rhythmic pattern as the sun's golden rays swept across it. The lovely voices of Tahitian singers and the ukulele's tunes filled the air, blending with the soft rustle of the palm palms.

Exotic flowers' fragrant smell teased the senses as it drifted across the streets.

The attraction of unspoiled beauty and undiscovered riches drew explorers and adventurists from far-off regions to Tahiti.

They were amazed when they traveled across the great ocean to see the craggy mountains towering magnificently from the turquoise seas. It seemed to them as if heaven itself had suddenly manifested.

Tahiti has a tale to be told at every turn. The revered Marae, antiquated stone temples built in honor of the gods, murmured stories of a bygone era.

Secrets of love and desire were spoken by the flowing waterfalls, whose waters danced down moss-covered rocks.

The vivid coral reefs, which were bustling with life below the water's surface, gave the impression of an unspoiled, pure planet.

But Tahiti's beauty went far beyond its aesthetic qualities. It was embodied in the spirit of the locals, who valued living in harmony with the natural world. The Tahitians cherished their land and water because they understood that they were a source of food.

They were skilled tattoo artists, marking their bodies with elaborate patterns that commemorated their ties to the soil and narrated the tales of their ancestors.

Time seemed to stand still in the center of Tahiti. Days were spent lazing in the sun's warm embrace, feasting on the island's mouthwatering fare, and taking part in jubilant dances to the mesmerizing rhythm of drums.

In this utopia, the idea of "hurry" had no place; instead, the Tahitians delighted in the simplicity of life and the value of savoring each moment.

The splendor of Tahiti changed as the sun fell below the horizon, illuminating the sky with shades of pink and orange.

Without the distraction of city lights, the night sky revealed a magnificent tapestry of stars, luring observers to daydream and consider the size of the cosmos.

It served as a gentle reminder that there could be wonder and awe even in a paradise.

With its immaculate beaches, towering mountains, and colorful culture, Tahiti was a place that not only delighted the senses but also fed the spirit.

It served as a haven where people could escape the turmoil of contemporary life and re-establish contact with its essential components.

Consequently, those who had the good fortune to feel Tahiti's embrace carried Tahiti's essence with them always.

Their hearts were imprinted with Tahiti's spirit, which kept luring them back to its beaches. They were eternally changed by the beauty of this entrancing island, a place where the ideals of paradise were realized.

Tahiti's attractiveness never lost its appeal as the years went by. Many people developed a wanderlust after hearing the tales and encounters of those who had traveled to the island, which spread widely. People yearned to experience Tahiti's magic firsthand from all corners of the world.

Travel became easier to obtain as the globe developed, connecting disparate regions and civilizations.

In order to bring travelers closer to Tahiti, a paradise that exists only in dreams, airlines have cut out routes across the skies and cruise ships have traveled over huge seas.

A magnificent but genuine experience is offered to guests by the resorts and eco-lodges that have sprung up, fitting in well with the island's natural splendor.

The true nature of Tahiti, however, remained unaltered throughout the expansion and change. The Tahitians persisted in upholding their customs and passing on their forefathers' knowledge to succeeding generations.

The old Marae served as a reminder of the island's rich spiritual past, providing a window into a time that has long since passed but is still highly loved.

Divers and snorkelers' imaginations were captured by the brilliant colors and variety of species of marine life that flourished in the protected coral reefs.

They were drawn into the water by the call of an underwater paradise, where beautiful sea turtles and lively dolphins danced side by side and schools of tropical fish filled the depths with their colorful splendor.

Exotic birds decorated the trees with bursts of vivid plumage as adventurers started out on trekking paths that wove through lush jungles.

They came to unnoticed waterfalls that plunged into sparkling pools and beckoned them to let the weight of the world wash away and lift their spirits.

They were enveloped by nature at these times, which brought comfort and a fresh feeling of awe.

Tahiti's appeal went beyond its natural splendors. Its residents welcomed guests into their thriving neighborhoods with their contagious friendliness and sincere grins.

Visitors were encouraged to join, and when they did so, the air was filled with traditional dances and music. They feasted lavishly, relishing the tastes of the island's richness as they ate exquisite fish, fragrant vanilla, and fresh tropical fruits.

A feeling of calm spread around the island as the sun fell below the horizon, illuminating the lagoons with a golden hue.

The mesmerizing chants of ancient rituals brought the night to life as tales of creation and togetherness were celebrated beneath a canopy of stars.

By telling their stories, the Tahitians helped to spread a deep understanding of the interconnectedness of all living things and the value of protecting the natural world.

Visitors found a feeling of harmony inside themselves in Tahiti's embrace of beauty. They were reminded of the natural simplicity and pleasure that awaited anyone who sought them in the world.

As a result, they returned from the island not only with photos and trinkets but also with a fresh viewpoint that served as a reminder to slow down, to appreciate the beauty of nature, and to create cross-cultural friendships.

The tale of Tahiti is still being told today, attracting souls and igniting aspirations. It continues to stand for the peaceful coexistence of humans and the natural environment.

The physical and spiritual beauty of the island continues to be a lasting tribute to the transformational power of nature and the limitless capacity that each of us has to preserve the havens that bless our planet.

TAHITI DAILY LIVING ROUTINE

The Polynesian island nation of Tahiti, which is renowned for its breathtaking natural beauty and dynamic culture, is recognized for its laid-back lifestyle and strong connection to the water.

Here is a typical routine that sums up daily life in Tahiti:

Morning:

To see the stunning Pacific Ocean dawn, get up early.

To start the day, go for a stroll along the beach or for a relaxing dip in the warm seas.

Enjoy a leisurely breakfast of papaya, pineapple, mango, and other tropical fruits from the area, along with freshly baked bread and coffee.

Mid-morning:

To peruse vibrant kiosks offering a range of tropical food, handicrafts, and souvenirs, visit the neighborhood market, such Le Marché de Papeete.

Discover the history and culture of the area by exploring Papeete, the region's capital, and stopping by major sights like the Marché Municipale, the Pearl Museum, or the Robert Wan Pearl Museum.

Enjoy a delicious lunch featuring Tahitian cuisine at noon.

Try a plate of fafaru, which is fish that has been fermented with vegetables and coconut cream, or sample poisson cru, a meal that is created with raw fish that has been marinated in lime juice and coconut milk.

After lunch, take a little nap or choose a shaded area on the beach to unwind and enjoy the sunshine.

Afternoon:

Participate in water sports like snorkeling, diving, or paddleboarding in the pristine lagoons. Tahiti is renowned for having beautiful coral reefs and a diverse marine population.

Discover lush rainforests, waterfalls, and picturesque vistas by going on an ATV tour or guided hike through the island's interior. Visit the

Fautaua Valley and its spectacular waterfall as soon as you can.

Evening: Take in a breathtaking sunset while walking along the beach or have a special meal at a restaurant by the water.

Try some traditional Tahitian fare like mahi-mahi, a native fish, or po'e, a dessert made with banana and arrowroot.

Attend a performance of a Polynesian dance style or a live music event that features ukulele, Tahitian drums, and stunning hula dances to fully experience the culture.

Enjoy a cool cocktail before going to bed that is made with regional ingredients like fresh tropical fruits, coconut, or Tahitian vanilla.

Embracing nature, taking in the ocean, indulging in delectable cuisine, and appreciating the rich Polynesian culture that gives Tahiti its distinctive character are all part of the island's daily routine.

CULTURAL VARIETY AND HISTORY

In French Polynesia, an archipelago in the South Pacific Ocean, Tahiti is the biggest and most populated island. Its centuries-long history and diverse cultural variety have created its identity.

Tahiti's history began more than a thousand years ago when Polynesians first made the island their home.

Although the precise origins of the early settlers are still up for debate among scholars, it is generally accepted that they came from Southeast Asia and navigated the vast Pacific Ocean using their prowess as seafarers.

British adventurer Samuel Wallis and French explorer Louis Antoine de Bougainville came in Tahiti in the 18th century, establishing the first European contacts with the island.

Following the arrival of additional explorers, traders, and missionaries, these encounters marked the start of European influence in Tahiti.

Tahiti was designated a French protectorate in 1842, and thereafter a French colony in 1880. French rule and influence during this time of colonialism influenced the language, legal framework, and educational institutions of Tahitian culture.

CULTURAL DIVERSITY

Tahiti is well known for its lively cultural variety, which has its roots in the Polynesian history of the island nation.

The Maohi, or native Tahitian culture, provides the basis of the island's identity and is still revered and honored today.

Strong relationships to the community and within the family are fundamental to traditional Tahitian society.

Tahitian culture is heavily influenced by dance and music, and there are enthralling shows that include popular dances like the 'ote'a and aparima as well as traditional melodies and drums.

Intricate woodcarvings, striking tattoos, and motifs on tapa fabric are some noteworthy examples of Tahitian art.

The deep ties that the Tahitian people have to their environment are reflected in the many depictions of nature, ancestral stories, and legendary beings in these artistic forms.

The cultural fabric includes the Tahitian language, also known as Reo Tahiti. Due to the country's colonial past, French is the official language; nevertheless, recent initiatives to maintain and revive Tahitian as a spoken language have led to a resurgence in Tahitian use.

The blending of many ethnic influences enhances Tahiti's already rich cultural variety. The island's population is made up of native Tahitians as well as individuals of European, Chinese, and other Polynesian ancestries.

A unique and diversified community where traditions, dialects, and customs coexist peacefully has been made possible by this mingling of cultures.

Tahiti is now a well-liked tourist destination, drawing travelers from all over the globe who come to take in the spectacular natural beauty, partake in water sports, and immerse themselves in the rich tapestry of Tahitian culture and history.

GEOGRAPHICAL LOCATION

LOCATION: Tahiti is located in the center of French Polynesia, about 4,000 km (2,500 miles) southeast of Hawaii and 7,900 km (4,900 miles) northwest of Sydney, Australia.

Tahiti is a member of the Society Islands, an archipelago made up of more than a dozen islands and atolls. French Polynesia is made up of five island groupings, one of which being the Society Islands.

Tahiti is divided into two main regions, Tahiti Iti and Tahiti Nui, which are both known as the "big Tahiti" and the "small Tahiti," respectively.

The bigger and more populated region is called Tahiti Nui, whereas Tahiti Iti is a tiny peninsula that is situated on the island's southeasterly edge.

MOUNTAINOUS TERRAIN: The island's spectacular, lush, and mountainous landscapes are due to its volcanic origins. At around 2,241 meters (7,352 feet) above sea level, Mount Orohena is the island's tallest mountain.

COASTAL FEATURES: A coral reef surrounds Tahiti, forming a lagoon that encircles the island.

Deep coves, rugged cliffs, and lovely beaches define the shoreline.

On Tahiti's northwest coast is where Papeete, the capital and biggest city of French Polynesia, is situated.

Tropical Tahiti is renowned for its abundant and varied flora. Coconut trees, other luxuriant plantations, and deep jungles dominate the whole island.

CLIMATE: Tahiti has a tropical climate with warm temperatures all year round. More rain falls during the wet season, which typically lasts from November to April. The dry season, on the other hand, lasts from May to October.

The most populated island in French Polynesia is Tahiti, which has a population of around 190,000. Urban regions, notably those in and around Papeete, are home to the bulk of the population.

TOURISM: Tahiti is a well-liked vacation spot, noted for its breathtaking natural beauty, pristine oceans, and abundant marine life. Swim, dive, surf, hike, and learn about the local culture are among the popular tourist pursuits.

TRANSPORTATION: The major entry point to French Polynesia is Tahiti's international airport, Faa'a International Airport, which is close to Papeete.

Additionally, the island has a network of roads connecting its various regions, facilitating transportation for both locals and visitors.

CLIMATE IN TAHITI

Warm temperatures are prevalent year-round in Tahiti. The average high temperature varies depending on the season, from 29°C (84°F) in the winter to 31°C (88°F) in the summer. All year round, the low temperature typically ranges from 23°C (73°F) to 24°C (75°F).

Tahiti receives a lot of precipitation, and there are rainy and dry seasons there. Heavy rainfall and sporadic tropical storms or cyclones are more frequent during the rainy season, which normally lasts from November to April.

Between May and October is the dry season, which has lower humidity and less precipitation.

Due to its tropical setting, Tahiti experiences high amounts of humidity all year round. The region's lush foliage and tropical atmosphere are influenced by the region's high average humidity of 80% or more.

Trade Winds: The east-bound trade winds have an impact on Tahiti. These breezes have a cooling impact and assist to control the temperatures, which improves the environment.

sunlight: Tahiti has a fair quantity of sunlight all year round, with 7 to 8 hours on average. However, during the rainy season, cloud cover may increase.

It's crucial to keep in mind that Tahiti and the other islands might experience varying climatic conditions depending on where you are. Furthermore, weather patterns can alter, so it's always a good idea to check the local weather forecast for the most accurate and up-to-date information before traveling to or planning activities in Tahiti.

Breathtaking Beauty: Tahiti is well known for its breathtaking natural beauty. White sand beaches, mountains covered in rich vegetation, and bright coral reefs surround the island. There are a ton of chances for adventure, discovery, and leisure in this gorgeous landscape.

Tahiti is renowned for having opulent overwater bungalows. With direct access to the water from your own terrace, these distinctive accommodations let you stay just over the lagoon.

A once-in-a-lifetime experience, staying in an overwater cottage provides unmatched vistas and a calm atmosphere.

Rich Culture: Polynesian customs are profoundly ingrained in the lively and diversified Tahitian culture. Visitors get the opportunity to experience local culture firsthand, see traditional dances, listen to lovely music, and take part in cultural activities.

A new depth is added to the journey by learning about Tahitian traditions and history.

Water Activities: Tahiti is a paradise for water lovers because to its crystal-clear seas and diverse marine life. Among the exhilarating sports you may take part in are deep-sea fishing, jet-skiing, sailing, snorkeling, and scuba diving.

Discovering the vibrant coral reefs and swimming with tropical fish, dolphins, and even whales is a once-in-a-lifetime experience.

Tahitian cuisine is a delicious blend of traditional Polynesian tastes, tropical fruits, and fresh seafood. Mahi-mahi, taro root, and tropical fruit sweets are a few examples of the local cuisine that provide a distinctive dining experience.

Another is poisson cru, which is raw fish marinated in coconut milk. Don't pass up the opportunity to sample authentic Tahitian cuisine while you are there.

Relaxation and serenity: Tahiti is the ideal location for anyone seeking peace and tranquility and an escape from the stress of everyday life. An environment of calm and renewal is created by the laid-back island vibe and the surrounding natural splendor.

Tahiti has several possibilities for relaxation, including beach time, spa treatments, and just taking in the quiet of the lagoon.

Outdoor activities and adventure: Tahiti offers a wide range of chances for outdoor exploration for those who are more daring vacationers.

Take a 4x4 safari trip, hike through lush jungles, travel to stunning waterfalls, or go on an exhilarating ATV adventure. Outdoor lovers will enjoy the island's untamed scenery and varied topography.

The mix of Tahiti's natural beauty, cultural diversity, and vast selection of activities make it the perfect vacation spot for anybody seeking a tropical escape.

When you visit Tahiti, the outside world disappears and is replaced with a tapestry of blue oceans, white sand beaches, and a warm "ia ora na" to greet you.

CHAPTER 1: WELCOME TO TAHITI

"Tahiti draws you in with its attraction of the tropics, giving a getaway to a paradise that seems like a dream come true."

I had an instantaneous feeling of peace as soon as I walked off the airport and into the beautiful island of Tahiti. My hair was softly ruffled by the warm wind, which was also loaded with the enticing aroma of tropical flowers.

I couldn't believe I was here, living the paradise of my dreams, at last.

My days in Tahiti were jam-packed with breathtaking excursions and indulgent downtime. My mornings were spent exploring the colorful coral reefs that were found under the calm seas.

I was struck speechless by the beauties of nature after snorkeling with vibrant fish and exquisite sea turtles.

I used to stroll along the immaculate white sand beaches in the late evenings, feeling the fine sand under my bare feet. I couldn't help but succumb to the turquoise waters' call to chill down.

I felt utterly at ease as I floated in the soft waves and gazed in awe at the spectacular scenery of the palm-lined shoreline.

My trip's highlight was a stop at Bora Bora, the South Pacific's crown gem. I set off on an enthralling boat tour of the island, exploring remote lagoons and secret coves.

The water's vivid hues of blue were unlike anything I had ever seen, and the dramatic Mount Otemanu towered majestically in the background, making for the ideal backdrop.

In Tahiti, the evenings were magical. I indulged in fresh fish and tropical fruits as I relished the mouthwatering aromas of traditional Polynesian meals.

I would seek out a peaceful place to see the captivating sunset as the sun dropped below the horizon, sending pink and orange colors over the sky, and I would be glad for the beauty that was all about me.

Tahiti was difficult to leave. My heart will always have the treasured experiences and memories I had created.

I made a promise to myself that I will visit this wonderful spot again one day as the jet lifted off as I gazed down at the beauty I was leaving behind.

My most recent vacation to Tahiti was an incredible experience filled with leisure, exploration, and the majesty of nature. It was a fantasy realized, and I am happy to have had the chance to visit such a paradise on Earth.

TAHITI's CAPITAL CITY

The biggest island in French Polynesia, Tahiti serves as the nation's political, social, and cultural hub. But Tahiti itself is not a nation; it is a part of French Polynesia, a French overseas territory.

On Tahiti's northwest coast sits Papeete, the nation of French Polynesia's capital.

The bigger of the two major islands that make up Tahiti, Tahiti Nui, is where Papeete is located. The city has a population of around 26,000 and is lively and active. The scenic harbor at Papeete, which serves as a significant port and a gathering place for yachts and cruise ships, is well recognized.

Papeete serves as the seat of several organizations' headquarters as well as housing for governmental agencies. In addition, it serves as French Polynesia's economic hub, hosting a variety of business ventures including banking, retail, and tourism.

French, Polynesian, and foreign influences are all present in the city. Traditional Polynesian architecture, contemporary structures, and bustling markets with fresh vegetables, seafood, and locally made crafts are all available for visitors to explore.

The Papeete Waterfront, a popular location for eating, shopping, and taking in the scenery, is located along the water.

With an international airport, Faa'a International Airport, only a few kilometers outside of the city, Papeete is well-linked. The main transit hub for people entering and leaving French Polynesia is this airport.

Papeete is an important administrative and commercial center in addition to being a center of culture. All through the year, it organizes a variety of cultural events, festivals, and exhibits that highlight the rich culture, music, dance, and visual arts of French Polynesia.

As the capital and entryway to French Polynesia, Papeete is a bustling and dynamic city that offers a unique combination of the region's natural beauty, cultural experiences, and modern conveniences.

REGIONS IN TAHITI

Although the word "Tahiti" is frequently used to describe the entire island, it is made up of several different regions, each of which has its attractions and activities. The major Tahitian areas are listed below:

The primary entryway to Tahiti is located in the capital city of French Polynesia, Papeete. It is a thriving urban hub that is a busy urban center and is situated on the northwest coast of the island.

Numerous stores, markets, eateries, and nightlife options can be found here. Historical locations including the Papeete Cathedral, the Presidential Palace, and the Museum of Tahiti and Her Islands may be found in Papeete.

Tahiti's international airport, Faa'a International Airport, is located in Faa'a, a town next to Papeete. Although mostly residential, it does have some hotels and other lodging options for visitors.

PUNAAUIA: Situated on Tahiti's west coast, Punaauia is renowned for its opulent hotels and stunning beaches. Numerous water sports, including jet skiing, diving, and snorkeling, are available in this area.

The Museum of Tahiti and Her Islands, which offers information on French Polynesia's history, culture, and natural environment, is one of Punaauia's top tourist destinations.

PAPARA: Situated on Tahiti's southwest coast, Papara is a well-liked vacation spot for surfers. It draws both residents and tourists since it has some of the island's top surf breaks.

Papara also has beautiful natural scenery, such as green mountains and beaches with black sand.

Mahina is a region on Tahiti's northeastern coast. It is renowned for its beautiful coastline landscape, which offers breathtaking views of the ocean and adjacent islands.

Point Venus, a notable location where Captain James Cook saw the transit of Venus in 1769, is also located near Mahina.

TAIARAPU: Situated on Tahiti's southern shore, Taiarapu is a location renowned for its unspoiled beaches, rocky coastline, and lush flora. It includes many districts, notably Teahupoo, well-known to surfers for its strong and difficult waves.

Taiarapu provides chances for horseback riding, hiking, and discovering Tahiti's stunning natural surroundings.

Teahupoo: One of the most difficult waves in the world, Teahupoo is a well-known surfing location in Tahiti. Teahupoo, which is surrounded by beautiful rainforests, draws skilled surfers who come to ride its famed barrels.

This location hosts the yearly Billabong Pro Tahiti, a World Surf League event.

RELIGIONS IN TAHITI

Christianity, primarily diverse Protestant and Roman Catholic groups, is the predominant religion practiced in Tahiti.

It is crucial to remember that many Tahitians still place importance on traditional Polynesian beliefs and rituals, sometimes known as "M'ohi" or "M'ohi beliefs," and that some of these ideas may be integrated into their Christian religion.

Beginning in the early 19th century, European missionaries brought Christianity to Tahiti.

Protestant denominations are common and have a sizable following, including the Protestant Reformed Church of French Polynesia (Église Protestante Ma'ohi).

A significant section of the population also practices Roman Catholicism, and the Roman Catholic Church is present on the islands.

Traditional Polynesian beliefs and traditions continue to be a part of Tahiti's cultural landscape in addition to Christianity.

The devotion of ancestral spirits and deities, as well as the idea of mana (spiritual force), are at the core of these beliefs.

The rites, practices, and ceremonies associated with M'ohi beliefs include the adoration of deities such as Ta'aroa (the creator god), Ta'ahua (the deity of riches), and Hina (the goddess of the moon).

It's important to keep in mind that Tahiti's religious landscape is varied, as it is in many other countries, and that there may be people there who worship other religions or pursue other spiritual paths.

However, Christianity, including its Roman Catholic and Protestant branches, and the persistence of traditional Polynesian beliefs and practices are the two main religious traditions in Tahiti.

TAHITI's SURROUNDING ISLANDS

Five archipelagos and 118 islands and atolls make up French Polynesia. The following islands encircle Tahiti:

MOOREA: Moorea, which lies northwest of Tahiti, is renowned for its breathtaking natural beauty, which includes verdant highlands, white sand beaches, and a beautiful coral reef.

BORA BORA: Northwest of Tahiti lies a place called Bora Bora, known for its renowned blue lagoon, opulent hotels, and overwater bungalows. It is regarded as one of the world's most beautiful islands.

RAIATEA: is known as the "Sacred Island" and is recognized as the cultural and historical center of French Polynesia. It is located to the west of Tahiti. It is a key location for conventional Polynesian navigation and the site of ancient marae (temples).

HUAHINE: Northwest of Tahiti, this island is known as the "Garden of Eden" for its lush vegetation, blue lagoons, and prehistoric monuments. It gives visitors a more unique experience.

TETIAROA: is a private atoll in the north of Tahiti that is renowned for its seclusion and natural splendor. A luxurious eco-resort has taken over what was once Marlon Brando's getaway.

TAHAA: West of Bora Bora lies a place named Tahaa, which is also known as the "Vanilla Island" because of its huge vanilla plantations. With fewer people, it provides a more sedate and genuine Polynesian experience.

CHAPTER 2: THE NATURAL BEAUTY OF TAHITI

"In Tahiti, the splendor of nature radiates like a live postcard. You are transported to a place of absolute enchantment by the lush valleys, immaculate beaches, and the warm embrace of the ocean, leaving an everlasting impression on your heart".

CRYSTAL CLEAR WATERS

Tahiti is well known for its breathtakingly pure seas and all-natural beauty. Tahiti, which lies in French Polynesia in the South Pacific, is a tropical haven that draws tourists from all over the globe.

Here are some details about Tahiti's waters, which are renowned for their clarity:

Lagoon: One of the island's biggest draws is the vivid blue lagoon that surrounds Tahiti.

The lagoon's relatively modest depth and clean waters let you glimpse the colorful coral reefs and a variety of marine creatures that are present below the surface.

Tahiti is home to a lot of coral gardens where you may swim or dive to learn more about the underwater environment.

You can see well in the crystal-clear waters, marvel at the vibrant coral formations, and swim next to a variety of tropical fish, sea turtles, and other marine life.

Despite being a separate island in French Polynesia, Bora Bora is frequently mistaken for Tahiti due to its proximity and growing popularity among tourists.

Bora Bora is famed for its top-notch resorts and its well-known lagoon, which is noted for its remarkably pure seas.

It is the perfect place to go swimming, snorkeling, or just to take in the beauty of the surroundings since the lagoon at Bora Bora is a magnificent sight with its many colors of blue.

Moorea is a neighboring island of Tahiti that is renowned for its pure seas and breathtaking scenery. The island has lovely bays and serene lagoons, so there are plenty of options to enjoy the crystal-clear waters by swimming, kayaking, or paddleboarding.

Motu Islands: Numerous motu islands, little islets with immaculate beaches and crystal-clear seas, surround Tahiti and its adjacent islands.

These remote locations provide an opportunity to repose in paradise, recline on the white beach, and take a plunge in the alluring turquoise seas.

FALKARAVA ATOLL

In the Tuamotu Archipelago, a region of French Polynesia in the South Pacific Ocean, the Fakarava Atoll is a magnificent coral atoll.

It is notably located in the Society Islands group, 450 kilometers (280 miles) northeast of Tahiti, French Polynesia's biggest island.

Known for its extraordinary natural beauty, the Fakarava Atoll is designated as a UNESCO Biosphere Reserve. With a lagoon size of around 1,112 square kilometers (429 square miles), it is the second-largest atoll in French Polynesia.

The lagoon is a well-liked location for divers and snorkelers because of the abundance of different marine life there, such as vibrant coral reefs, tropical fish, and even sharks.

The atoll is made up of many islets, the two largest of which are Fakarava and Tetamanu. The bigger of the two, Fakarava, acts as the administrative hub, while Tetamanu is renowned for its lovely beach and ancient coral church.

Fakarava Atoll also has a calm, laid-back ambiance that is ideal for individuals seeking leisure and a vacation from the busy city life, in addition to its natural features.

It offers a chance to encounter genuine Polynesian culture and friendliness.

Travelers may reach Fakarava Atoll by flying domestically to the Fakarava Airport, which is situated on the main islet, from Tahiti.

When you arrive, you may explore the atoll's unspoiled beaches, go diving or snorkeling in the lagoon, tour the lovely towns, or just relax and take in the tranquil atmosphere of this tropical paradise.

Fakarava Atoll in Tahiti is a genuine jewel of the South Pacific, providing tourists with a unique and memorable experience among breathtaking natural beauty and abundant marine species.

THE LAGOONARIUM

A well-liked tourist destination on the island of Moorea in French Polynesia is the lagoonarium in Tahiti, also called the Moorea Lagoonarium.

Visitors get the chance to see and interact with a variety of marine animals in this unusual open-water aquarium.

Due to the Lagoonarium's location in a shallow lagoon, guests may enjoy the splendor of the underwater environment without the need for scuba or snorkeling gear. For both visitors and aquatic life, it offers a secure and regulated environment.

A variety of activities are available for visitors to the Lagoonarium, including swimming with sharks and rays, feeding and viewing tropical fish, and learning about marine ecology from professional guides.

Sea turtles, tropical fish, brilliant coral, sharks, and rays are just a few of the many aquatic creatures that call the lagoon home.

Marine conservation and education are the main goals of the Lagoonarium. It attempts to promote sustainable practices and create awareness of how critical it is to conserve the delicate maritime habitat.

Through guided tours and educational programs, visitors can find out more about the efforts being made to protect the environment and marine life.

Visitors may explore and take in the breathtaking marine richness of the seas of French Polynesia in a unique and immersive way at the Lagoonarium in Tahiti.

MOUNT OROHENA

The island of Tahiti is home to Mount Orohena, the highest mountain in French Polynesia. It is a well-known landmark in the neighborhood with spectacular views that draw plenty of tourists who want to hike and discover the local natural beauty.

A few important facts regarding Mount Orohena are as follows:

Height: The highest peak in French Polynesia is Mount Orohena, which rises to a towering 2,241 meters (7,352 feet) above sea level.

Location: It is located on the island of Tahiti's central region, which is where the majority of French Polynesia's people live and where the island is the biggest. Located in the Tahiti Nui area, the mountain is a piece of the volcanic chain that created Tahiti.

Access and Hiking: For those who like the great outdoors, hiking Mount Orohena is a favorite pastime. The ascent is difficult and calls for high physical condition and planning.

For reasons of safety and navigation, it is advised to hire a local guide or sign up for a scheduled trip. Before starting the journey, it's necessary to be prepared and knowledgeable since the terrain may be challenging and rough, and the weather might change suddenly.

Flora and fauna: Mount Orohena is renowned for having a diverse array of life. Rainforests with a diversity of native plant species are abundant on the lower slopes.

More rocky landscapes will surround you as you climb, and the greenery will grow sparser. Numerous bird species, including the critically endangered Tahiti monarch, call the mountain home.

Views & Scenery: Hikers who conquer Mount Orohena are rewarded with breathtaking panoramic views of Tahiti and the other islands.

The gorgeous shoreline, colorful coral reefs, and great expanse of the Pacific Ocean are all visible on clear days. The scenery is really beautiful and extremely motivating.

It is crucial to get the most recent information, speak with local officials or tour guides, and make sure you have the right equipment and permissions if you want to visit Mount Orohena or undertake the walk.

Outdoor activity safety should always come first, particularly in treacherous terrain like mountains.

INLET OF MATAVIA

French Polynesia in the South Pacific Ocean is home to the tiny coral atoll known as Mataiva Atoll.

It is a member of the Tuamotu Archipelago and is located about 270 km (168 miles) northeast of Tahiti, the biggest and most populated island in French Polynesia.

Natural splendor, immaculate beaches, and an abundance of marine life may all be found at Mataiva Atoll.

There is a tiny population living on the atoll, which is made up of a ring of coral reefs around a lagoon. Pahua, the atoll's principal hamlet, can be found on the island's southwest side.

In the crystal-clear lagoon waters of Mataiva Atoll, visitors may engage in sports like snorkeling, diving, and fishing.

The atoll is surrounded by a marine environment that is rich in biodiversity, home to bright coral reefs and many different types of tropical fish, making it a well-liked vacation spot for divers.

Mataiva Atoll is governed by the French government since it is a part of French Polynesia.

Tahitian is also commonly spoken by locals, however, French is the official language.

The atoll is reachable by boat or light plane, and a few guesthouses and lodging options are offered to travelers.

CHAPTER 3: MAKING TRAVEL

"Traveling is more than simply getting there; it's also about enjoying the adventure itself."

SEASON TO VISIT

The dry season, usually from May through October, is the ideal time to go to Tahiti. The best weather is present at this time, with fewer showers, reduced humidity, and cooler temperatures.

The ideal range for outdoor activities and experiencing Tahiti's breathtaking scenery and beaches is between 70°F (21°C) to 85°F (29°C), on average.

It's crucial to remember that Tahiti has a tropical climate, so even in the dry season, there may still be sporadic rains.

A greater risk of rainfall, including tropical storms and cyclones, higher temperatures, and increased humidity are all characteristics of the wet season, which lasts from November to April.

Although the wet season may have lower prices and fewer visitors, because of the unpredictability of the weather, it might not be the best time for outdoor activities.

The greatest time to visit Tahiti is between June and August since the water clarity is usually at its finest during these months. If you want to go diving or snorkeling, these are the best things to do while there.

However, these months also happen to fall during the busiest travel period, so you might run into more people and pay more for lodging and travel.

TRAVEL AND ENTRY REQUIREMENTS

You must make sure you have the required travel paperwork and entrance criteria before visiting Tahiti, which is a part of French Polynesia.

The following broad recommendations are provided, although for the most recent information, it is always advised to contact the appropriate authorities or your local embassy or consulate:

Passport: To enter Tahiti, you must have a current passport. Ensure your passport is valid for at least six more months than the length of time you want to remain.

Visa: For visits of up to 90 days, citizens of countries that are a member of the European Union, the United States, Canada, Australia, or New Zealand are exempt from obtaining a visa.

But you might need a visa if you're a citizen of another nation. For information on visa requirements, contact the French embassy or consulate in your country of residence.

Return Ticket: To demonstrate your desire to depart Tahiti within the allotted duration, you often need to have a return or onward ticket.

Entry Form: You must fill out an entry form known as the "ETIS" (Electronic Travel Information System) before departing for Tahiti.

This form asks for data regarding your trip, such as your contact information, lodging preferences, and medical history. It is often filled out online, and you will need to have the form's confirmation with you when you arrive.

Proof of Accommodation: You may need to provide documentation of your lodging when visiting Tahiti. This may be shown by hotel bookings, a letter of invitation from the host, or any other document that attests to the specifics of your lodging.

Travel insurance: Although it is not required, it is strongly advised to obtain travel insurance that covers medical costs and emergencies when visiting Tahiti. This will provide you with financial security in the event of unanticipated events.

Health Requirements: Tahiti does not have any further immunization requirements beyond the previously listed COVID-19 criteria. To be safe, it's best to stay current on normal vaccines and discuss any suggested travel immunizations with a medical expert.

Tahiti adheres to French customs laws as it is a part of French Polynesia. When entering the country, be aware of restricted and prohibited items, such as specific foods, plants, or animal products. To prevent any problems at customs, make sure you are aware of these rules.

The French Pacific Franc (CFP) is Tahiti's official unit of exchange. For modest transactions or scenarios where credit cards may not be accepted, it is advised to keep some local cash on hand. The majority of hotels, eateries, and tourist destinations accept credit cards.

Travel Advice: Before your journey, it's important to review the travel advice for French Polynesia given by the government of your own country.

This will provide you with information on any travel advisories, security issues, or particular instructions to follow while you're there.

USEFUL TRAVEL ADVICE

LOCAL TRANSIT: Become familiar with the available local transit alternatives, including taxis, buses, trains, and trams. Know their times, routes, and prices. For more convenient travel, think about purchasing a transit pass or card.

LANGUAGE: Acquire a few fundamental expressions in the native tongue, such as "hello," "thank you," and "where are we?" This will enable you to interact with the community and appreciate their culture.

CURRENCY: Research the exchange rates and local currency. Find places where you may withdraw money, such as ATMs or currency exchange agencies. To prevent any problems with your cards, let your bank know about your trip intentions.

SAFETY: Do some research on the level of safety at your location. Take the required safeguards after identifying any possible threats, such as danger zones or frequent con artists. Secure your belongings, and pay attention to your surroundings.

LOCAL CUSTOMS AND ETIQUETTE: To respect local culture, get familiar with local customs, traditions, and etiquette.

This covers proper greetings, body language, and attire, as well as any taboo or delicate subjects to steer clear of.

WEATHER: Check the weather prediction for your destination during the dates you will be traveling. Remember to bring comfortable attire and accessories.

Depending on the predicted weather, think about taking an umbrella, sunscreen, or warm clothing.

TOURIST ATTRACTIONS: Learn about the top monuments, museums, parks, and historical places in the area where you plan to go. Consider opening times, entrance costs, and any special events or exhibits when making your schedule.

EXPLORE THE LOCAL CUISINE and sample some traditional fare. Look into well-known neighborhood eateries or street food sellers that residents or internet reviewers have suggested. Take into account any food allergies or limitations you may have.

HEALTH AND SAFETY'S: Learn about any immunizations or safety measures that may be necessary for your travel location. Bring any required prescriptions, as well as travel protection. In case of crises, locate the closest clinics or hospitals.

Check the local customs laws at your destination to make sure you abide by any limitations on things like food, trinkets, or technology. By doing this, you may travel without experiencing any inconveniences or legal problems.

MONEY AND CURRENCY ISSUES

The French Pacific Franc (CFP Franc) is the official currency of Tahiti, the biggest island in French Polynesia. Several of France's overseas territories, including Tahiti, use the CFP Franc as their official currency.

It is locked at a fixed exchange rate to the euro and has the currency code XPF.

The following are some essential details concerning money and currencies in Tahiti:

Currency Exchange: In Tahiti, banks, currency exchange agencies, and certain hotels provide CFP Franc exchange for major world currencies including the US Dollar and Euro.

To obtain the greatest value, it's a good idea to compare exchange rates and costs.

Credit cards and ATMs are both readily accessible in Tahiti's main cities and tourism hubs. Hotels, eateries, and bigger institutions all take credit cards like Visa and Mastercard.

Nevertheless, it's wise to always have some cash on hand, especially in more rural and smaller towns.

Traveler's checks are typically accepted in Tahiti, however, their use has decreased over time. For your financial requirements, it can be more practical to carry a combination of cash and cards.

Cost of living: Tahiti is renowned for having a high cost of living, particularly when compared to France's mainland. The price of lodging, eating out, and activities may be more expensive than usual. It's advised to organize your spending and set a realistic budget.

Tipping: Since service fees are often included in the bill in Tahiti, tipping is not common there. However, if you experience exceptional service, you are welcome to round up the bill or leave a small gratuity as a mark of appreciation.

Banks in Tahiti are typically open from 7:30 AM to 3:30 PM, Monday through Friday. Several banks might close for lunch.

It's crucial to remember that bank hour might change, so it's best to confirm them with the particular bank branch.

Taxes: Tahiti imposes a value-added tax (VAT) on products and services known as the "Taxe sur la Valeur Ajoutée" (TVA). The standard rate at the moment is 5%. In most cases, VAT is included in the prices listed in shops and restaurants.

Foreign Currency Restrictions: Bringing foreign money into Tahiti is not prohibited. However, it is advised to declare large sums of cash when you arrive if you are carrying them.

Before leaving for Tahiti, it's a good idea to check with your bank or financial institution to let them know about your trip plans and make sure your cards will function normally while there.

TIPS & PRECAUTIONS FOR SAFETY'S

Your safety should always come first when you travel, and you should always take care to make your trip safe and comfortable.
Following are some general safety recommendations and measures for travelers:

Do your homework before you go: Before you travel, do your homework. Learn about the local laws, traditions, and any dangers or security issues. Keep up with any government-issued travel warnings.

Invest in comprehensive travel insurance that includes coverage for personal liability, trip cancellation, and medical costs. Be careful to read and comprehend the policy's terms and conditions.

Protect your possessions: At all times, keep your valuables, including cash, credit cards, passports, and devices, safe. To keep your valuables near to you, think about wearing a money belt or neck pouch.

Displaying pricey products that can draw attention is best avoided.

Tell someone you can trust about your vacation plans: Let them know your itinerary. Share your itinerary, including information on your flights, lodging, and any planned activities.

Maintain frequent contact with them, particularly if your plans alter.

Be alert to your surroundings and use caution, particularly in congested locations, popular destinations, and public transit. Keep an eye out for unusual conduct, and alert the police or your hotel if you have any worries.

Use reputable modes of transportation: Go with authorized taxis, ride-sharing services, or authorized airport shuttles. Be cautious of pickpockets and keep an eye on your stuff while utilizing public transit.

Even though it's fun to meet new people when traveling, use care while engaging with strangers. To someone you've just met, don't divulge personal information or specifics about your trip or lodging arrangements.

Avoid huge public meetings, rallies, or protests: These events should be avoided since they sometimes become violent or rapidly get out of hand. Keep an eye on regional news and heed local officials' advice.

Take the appropriate steps to protect your health, such as getting vaccinated before a trip and packing any required medicines.

To avoid foodborne infections, drink bottled water in locations with uncertain water quality and abide by food safety regulations.

Secure your lodging: Opt for trustworthy and secure lodging. Use the offered safes or lockers to keep your valuables. To increase security, think about adding a door wedge or a portable alarm.

Maintain contact: When traveling, have a dependable communication method. Keep your phone charged at all times, and be familiar with the local emergency numbers. Keep a list of crucial contacts, such as those at your consulate or embassy.

Be careful while utilizing public Wi-Fi networks since they could not be safe. Practice proper cybersecurity.

Avoid using public networks to access sensitive information, such as online banking or personal accounts. To increase security, use a virtual private network (VPN).

BUDGETING A TRIP TO TAHITI

To make the most of your holiday and have a clear idea of your spending, creating a budget for your trip to Tahiti is essential. When setting a budget for a trip to Tahiti, keep the following points in mind:

Flights: Examine Tahiti flight costs from your starting point. Depending on the airline, the season, and how far in advance you buy, flight tickets may cost a lot of money.

When calculating your flight costs, be sure to account for any additional fees, such as baggage fees or seat selection.

Tahiti provides a variety of lodging alternatives, from opulent resorts to reasonably priced guesthouses

. Choose the kind of lodging that best fits your needs and price range. Consider things like location, facilities, and reviews when doing pricing research.

Travel: Renting a vehicle in Tahiti is a common way to get to the islands. Consider fuel costs, parking fees, and any additional insurance or fees when comparing car rental prices.

As an alternative, you may depend on organized excursions, taxis, or public transit, each of which may have additional charges.

Meals: Eating out in Tahiti may be pricey, particularly at upscale eateries. Plan your meals properly and take a variety of dining alternatives into account, such as eating at local restaurants and, if feasible, self-catering.

Additionally, you can browse the neighborhood markets for inexpensive snacks and fresh food.

Tahiti provides a variety of excursions and activities, including boat cruises, hiking, diving, and snorkeling. Determine the costs of the experiences you're interested in, then set aside some money for them.

Shopping and Souvenirs: If you want to go shopping or purchase any souvenirs during your vacation, allocate money for these costs.

It's a good idea to study normal pricing for the things you're interested in as prices might fluctuate.

Consider buying travel insurance to safeguard yourself against unforeseen circumstances like trip cancellation, medical problems, or misplaced baggage.

To include this expense in your budget, investigate several insurances and their pricing.

Miscellaneous Expenses: Don't forget to set aside money for unanticipated costs like tips, local taxes, Wi-Fi fees, and any other charges that may occur while you're traveling.

It's crucial to keep in mind that the price of a vacation to Tahiti might vary significantly based on your travel choices, how long you stay, and the activities you decide to partake in.

You may make a reasonable travel budget by doing pricing research, evaluating your alternatives, and preparing ahead of time.

CHAPTER 4; HEALTH INFORMATION.

"To fully appreciate Tahiti's splendor, you must lead a balanced lifestyle. Keep in mind to hydrate under the hot tropical sun and to fuel your body with fresh local produce and the delectable cultural heritage of Polynesian cuisine. As it benefits your general health and well-being, take some time to unwind and embrace island life's slower pace".

Tahiti's medical centers

French Polynesia's main island, Tahiti, contains several healthcare facilities that are open to both locals and tourists. A few of Tahiti's most important medical institutions are listed below:

Center Hospitalier de la Polynésie Française (CHPF): The Center Hospitalier de la Polynésie Française is Tahiti's primary medical facility.

It is situated in the capital city of Papeete and offers a variety of medical services, including emergency care, surgery, specialist treatments, and diagnostics.

Clinique Paofai is a private medical facility in Papeete that provides a range of healthcare services, including consultations, laboratory testing, imaging, and minor surgical operations.

Clinique Cardella is a private clinic with an emphasis on cardiology and cardiovascular surgery that is located in Papeete. Including diagnostics, interventions, and post-operative care, it offers complete cardiac care.

Located in Pirae, a little town west of Papeete, is the public hospital known as Hopital du Taaone.

These include departments for children, gynecology, and ophthalmology along with general medical services, emergency care, and other specialty areas.

Clinique Paofai Mahina: This private clinic, which is based in Mahina, offers a range of medical services, such as consultations, lab work, imaging, and minor surgical operations.

Dentists and Clinics: Several dental clinics in Tahiti provide both general and specialty dental treatments, including examinations, cleanings, fillings, extractions, orthodontics, and oral surgery.

Tahitian Health System

The French healthcare system has had a significant impact on French Polynesia, a French overseas territory. Having both public and private healthcare providers distinguishes the French Polynesian healthcare system.

The Social Security Fund, or CPS, which is the primary source of health insurance in French Polynesia, offers public healthcare services.

For those living in French Polynesia, the CPS pays a substantial percentage of their medical costs. It's crucial to remember that the breadth of the coverage and the nature of the services offered might change.

Private healthcare facilities may be found in French Polynesia in addition to state healthcare services. The prices of services provided by private hospitals, clinics, and doctors are often higher than those provided by the CPS.

Many reasons, such as shorter wait times and access to specialized care, may influence some people to choose private healthcare.

It is recommended that both locals and guests in French Polynesia, including Tahiti, have complete health insurance coverage.

In addition to providing financial security in the case of unforeseen medical costs, this may assist assure access to a wider choice of healthcare services.

It's important to note that healthcare systems may develop and alter over time; thus, for the most up-to-date and accurate information about the healthcare system in the area, it's advised to examine updated and trustworthy sources or get in touch with local authorities or healthcare providers in Tahiti.

ADVICE ON TRAVELING HEALTH

To guarantee a safe and healthy journey, it's crucial to keep certain points in mind when it comes to travel health advice. The following suggestions are general:

Consult a healthcare expert: It is recommended to speak with a healthcare professional or travel medicine specialist before going, particularly to distant countries.

They may provide you with individualized guidance based on your travel plans, medical background, and particular requirements.

Verify that you are up to date on all of your normal vaccines. Also, find out if any vaccinations are suggested or required for the area you're traveling to. Vaccination records, including those for yellow fever, may be required by certain governments before entrance.

Do some homework before you go: Learn about any health concerns that may be present in the area where you want to vacation. Examine the local area for any endemic or emerging illnesses, as well as any particular health issues.

For this information, the websites of the World Health Organization (WHO) and the Centers for Disease Control and Prevention (CDC) are both excellent sources.

Medication & prescriptions: If you regularly use medications, be sure to pack enough for the length of your vacation. Keep copies of your prescriptions with you and carry your drugs in their original packaging.

It's a good idea to check if carrying certain prescriptions into the country where you're traveling is permitted.

Vacation insurance: Take into account getting medical coverage while acquiring travel insurance. If you become sick or have an accident while traveling, this might be helpful.

The coverage limitations and any exclusions should be understood by carefully reading the policy.

Safety while consuming food and water: Be careful what you eat and drink. In certain areas, it's advised to consume bottled or boiling water, stay away from raw or undercooked meats, and peel fruits and vegetables before eating them.

Consider using hand sanitizers or washing your hands often with soap and water.

Protect yourself against insects by taking the right precautions in locations where there is a chance of contracting a disease from a mosquito, such as malaria, dengue fever, or the Zika virus.

This can include using insect repellent, wearing long sleeves and trousers, and reserving lodgings with appropriate window screens or bed nets.

Sun protection: Wearing sunscreen with a high SPF, using hats and sunglasses, and looking for cover at the height of the sun's rays can shield you from the sun's damaging rays. Even in chilly or cloudy conditions, this is crucial.

Drink plenty of water and keep moving to avoid dehydration and circulation problems that may arise from long flights or other forms of travel.

During lengthy flights or car rides, stay hydrated by getting enough water, abstain from drinking too much alcohol, and get up and stretch occasionally.

Traveler's to Tahiti: Health Precautions

It's crucial to follow a few healthcare best practices if you're considering a vacation to Tahiti to travel safely and in good health. In Tahiti, the following health advice is provided for visitors:

Travel insurance: Before leaving on your vacation, ensure sure you have complete travel insurance that includes medical costs, emergency evacuation, and repatriation coverage.

You'll have financial security as a result in the event of any unanticipated medical crises.

Consult your doctor or a travel clinic to find out if any shots are advised or necessary for your trip to Tahiti. Hepatitis A and B, typhoid, and influenza vaccinations are routine for travelers. Aside from that, make sure you have all of your regular vaccinations.

Protection against mosquitoes: Zika and dengue viruses, among others, are spread by the insects that inhabit Tahiti.

Wear long sleeves and trousers, apply insect repellents with DEET in them, and remain in places with air conditioning or windows and doors that have screens on them if you want to be safe.

If your lodging is not sufficiently protected, you may also think about utilizing a bed net.

Sun protection is important since Tahiti has a tropical environment with intense sun exposure.

Apply sunscreen with a high SPF, find shade during the height of the sun's rays, and cover up with a hat and sunglasses to shield your skin from damaging UV rays.

In Tahiti's hot and muggy climate, it's extremely important to stay hydrated by drinking plenty of water. Dehydration may be prevented by carrying a water bottle with you and avoiding excessive alcohol use.

Food and Water Safety: Drink only bottled water and only use it to wash your teeth to avoid contracting a foodborne disease. Choose freshly prepared, hot meals instead of eating anything uncooked or undercooked.

When eating street food, exercise caution and make sure it is prepared and served hygienically.

Medication and First Aid Kit: If you regularly use prescription drugs, be sure to pack enough for the length of your vacation.
Put together a basic first aid box with the necessities, including bandages, antiseptic wipes, painkillers, antidiarrhea medicine, and any personal drugs that could be required.

Traveler's diarrhea: Use hand sanitizers or often wash your hands with soap and water to reduce the chance of getting a traveler's diarrhea by maintaining proper hand hygiene.

Except for fruits and vegetables that you can peel yourself, stay away from tap water, ice cubes, and uncooked produce.

Consult a doctor if you have any health questions: If you experience any health issues while visiting Tahiti, contact a doctor right away. For help, speak to your travel insurance company or the neighborhood emergency services.

Tahiti's Traditional Medicine and Cultural Health Practices

Tahiti, a French Polynesian island, is well-known for its rich cultural legacy and traditional traditions, particularly those that pertain to health and well-being. In Tahiti, the following cultural and traditional health practices are typical:

Tahitian Traditional Medicine: Tahitians have traditionally depended on traditional medical procedures that entail the use of local plants, herbs, and natural treatments to treat a range of illnesses. The so-called "tohunga," or traditional healers, are very knowledgeable about the regional flora and their therapeutic characteristics.

Massage and bodywork are highly valued in Tahitian culture for their relaxing and therapeutic properties. One well-liked method is referred to as "Taurumi," a conventional Tahitian massage that includes rhythmic motions, intense pressure, and the application of scented oils obtained from indigenous flora.

Plant-based Treatments: Tahitians employ a broad variety of plants and herbs for their healing qualities. These include Tiare (Gardenia tahitensis), which is well-known for its calming and healing properties, and noni (Morinda citrifolia), used for its purported anti-inflammatory and antioxidant effects.

Traditional Diet: Locally grown foods including fish, breadfruit, taro, and coconuts are used in traditional Tahitian cuisine. It is thought that eating this diet, which is high in important nutrients, will improve your general health and well-being.

Spiritual practices: In Tahitian culture, the relationship between the spiritual and physical selves is quite strong.

It is said that the rituals, dances, and music used in traditional celebrations, like the "Heiva" festival, help to develop harmony between the body, mind, and spirit.

Traditional Healers: In Tahitian society, the tohunga, also known as traditional healers, have a big part to play.

They have a specific understanding of traditional medicine and often provide therapies, direction, and counsel to those looking for all-natural cures for their health problems.

Respect for Nature: Tahitians have a strong connection to nature and trust in its curative powers. This includes activities like spending time outdoors and developing a close connection with the environment. It also includes practices like going to the beach.

While Tahiti values its traditional ways of doing things, it's crucial to remember that some modern medical services and facilities are accessible and frequently used.

To promote their health and well-being, many Tahitians combine ancient and contemporary methods, realizing the advantages of both.

EMERGENCY CONTACTS AND RESOURCES

Following are some crucial numbers and resources you should be aware of in Tahiti in case of an emergency:

Police services are available 24/7 by dialing 17.

Call the emergency hotline for medical services at (15), if there are any medical emergencies. If you need an ambulance, the emergency services will send one.

When a fire emergency arises, call the fire department at (18).
When a marine emergency arises, call the Coast Guard at (16).

Hospital: Tahiti's primary hospital is the Centre Hospitalier de Polynésie Française (CHPF). The nation's capital, Papeete, is where it is situated.

Call or email information the following address in French Polynesia: BP 3028 - 98713 Papeete-Tahiti
Phone: +689 40 50 50 50
www.chpf.pf is the website address.

It's crucial to keep in mind that hospital employees and emergency care providers may not always speak English, so it's best to have someone on hand who speaks French or to have a translation on hand in case one becomes required.

You should also get in touch with your embassy or consulate in French Polynesia for support in case of an emergency if you're a guest. In challenging circumstances, they may provide assistance and direction.

These helpful resources can be used in non-emergency situations:

Gendarmerie Nationale's Tourist Police: The Gendarmerie Nationale offers assistance to travelers. In addition to offering typical tourist information, they may give directions and assist with missing passports.

Phone: +689 40 54 16 55
French Polynesia's Papeete is located at Bâtiment Léontine - Boulevard Pomare IV.
United States Embassy in French Polynesia:

Phone: +689 40 50 52 00

The following address is in Papeete, French Polynesia: Centre Tamanu Iti - Punaauia - BP 10103
Website: http://pf.usembassy.gov

It's wise to get acquainted with the area's emergency services and available resources before visiting any location.

CHAPTER 5: GETTING AROUND TAHITI

"In Tahiti, getting about is like dancing on a wave; follow the island's beat."

IN TAHITI, TRANSPORTATION

There are several transportation choices for both inhabitants and tourists on Tahiti, the biggest island in French Polynesia. Listed below are Tahiti's main transportation options:

Flying: Tahiti has a major airport named Faa'a International Airport (PPT), which is not far from the nation's capital, Papeete. For visitors coming from all over the globe, it serves as the primary entry point.

Regular flights from and to Tahiti are run by several different airlines, linking them with significant locations in the Pacific, North America, Europe, and Asia.

Air Tahiti offers domestic flights that may be used to go to other islands in French Polynesia. In addition to connecting to several islands, including Bora Bora, Moorea, Huahine, Raiatea, and others, Air Tahiti operates a significant network of flights.

Ferries: Tahiti residents often choose to travel between its islands via ferries. Between Moorea, which is close by, to Tahiti, the firm Aremiti runs frequent boat services. 30 minutes or so are spent on the boat ride.

In Tahiti, especially in the Papeete region, taxis are readily accessible. They are available at hotels, tourist hotspots, and airports. Negotiate the fare before boarding the cab or insist that the driver utilize the meter.

Rental automobiles: Driving your vehicle in Tahiti is a practical option. Both the airport and Papeete both have several automobile rental companies. You should be aware that in French Polynesia, driving is done on the right side of the road.

Bus System: Tahiti has a bus system known as "Le Truck." The island is serviced by these vibrant buses, which run routes that pass through the main cities and tourist hotspots. Their timetables may be erratic, so it's best to make plans in advance even if they are an inexpensive alternative for transportation.

Bicycles and Scooters: Renting bicycles or scooters is a common way to get to the island, particularly for short trips or local exploration. These services are provided by several rental companies, and they may be a good way to take in Tahiti's picturesque splendor.

Although there are public transit choices, they could be less common in farther-flung places. Considering your schedule and preferences, it is usually a good idea to organize your transportation in advance.

A Rental Car for Tahiti Exploration

The cost of rent in Tahiti and the rental car market
In Tahiti, the starting rate for a basic budget automobile rental is normally approximately 6,000 XPF (French Pacific Francs) per day. Larger automobiles, SUVs, and expensive cars may have a higher price tag.

Additionally, you might need to budget for extra expenses like fuel, insurance, and any extras you might need like a GPS or child seat.

It is important to keep in mind that Tahiti and French Polynesia are often more costly holiday destinations. Because of the region's distant location and logistical difficulties, prices for products and services are often higher there than in other regions of the globe.

So it's a good idea to plan your spending accordingly and look into your options for renting a car to find the best deal for your needs and preferences.

Don't forget to review the rental agreement's terms and conditions, which should include information on insurance coverage, mileage limitations, and any other charges or prerequisites.

Before renting a car in Tahiti, it's also crucial to have a driver's license that is currently valid and be knowledgeable of the country's driving laws and guidelines.

Tahiti's Traffic Laws And Advice

Driving Permit: To drive in Tahiti, you'll need both your national driver's license and an active international driving permit (IDP). Ensure that you have both paperwork with you at all times when driving.

The right side of the road is where you should be driving in Tahiti, just as in France. On the left side of the car is where the driver sits.

In general, Tahiti has the following speed limits:

Cities: 50 km/h (31 mph)

60 mph (90 km/h) on open highways

110 km/h (68 mph), on highways

The stated speed restrictions should always be adhered to, however, since they may differ in certain places.

All passengers must always use seat belts while traveling in a car.

Children must be securely restrained in booster seats or child seats that are suitable for their age, height, and weight if they are traveling with young children.

Depending on the age of the kid, there could be different special needs.

Drugs and Alcohol: Tahiti has a 0.5 g/L (0.05%) blood alcohol limit for drivers. While driving, it is best to completely avoid using any type of intoxicant.

Handheld cell phones: It is completely forbidden to use a cell phone while driving. If you need to make or receive calls, use a hands-free device.

Road Conditions: Tahiti has a mixture of well-maintained roads and those that may be less developed, particularly in more isolated places. In rural areas, in particular, be prepared for twisting, narrow roads.

Parking: In cities, abide by the rules and signage that govern parking. Do not restrict other cars' access or park in no-parking areas.

Driving Defensively: As road conditions might change, practice defensive driving strategies. Be extra cautious around bicycles, motorbikes, and pedestrians in metropolitan areas.

Before you begin driving in Tahiti, become familiar with the meanings of the most frequent road signs. French is the primary language of traffic signs in French Polynesia.

Companies that I recommend for car rentals

A well-known worldwide automobile rental business has a location in Tahiti called Avis.

They provide easy pick-up and drop-off places at the Faa'a International Airport and various areas throughout the island and have a large fleet of cars available, including sedans, SUVs, and vans.

Another reputable automobile rental business that has operations in Tahiti is Europcar. They provide a wide variety of automobiles, such as 4x4s, premium automobiles, and compact cars.

Additionally, for your convenience, Europcar offers airport pickup and drop-off services.

Hertz Tahiti: Hertz is a well-known international name in the rental vehicle industry, and it also has operations there. Compact cars, SUVs, and minivans are among the many vehicles they provide to meet a range of requirements. In addition to other well-known Tahiti sites, Hertz offers pick-up and drop-off services at the Faa'a International Airport.

Budget Tahiti: Tahiti is home to one of the most well-known automobile rental companies. Economy cars, sedans, and SUVs are among the variety of vehicles they provide.

It is advantageous for visitors coming to Tahiti that Budget provides a pickup and drop-off site at the Faa'a International Airport.

Tahiti is only one of several places throughout the globe where the well-known vehicle rental company Enterprise has operations.

For various travel requirements, they provide a variety of cars. Among other places on the island, Enterprise offers services at the Faa'a International Airport.

It's wise to compare pricing, browse through user reviews, and examine the particular policies of each rental business before making a reservation. To guarantee vehicle availability, it is also advised to make reservations in advance, particularly during periods of high travel demand.

Tahiti's well-traveled roads and current road conditions

Boucle de Tahiti (Tahiti Ring Road): The Tahiti Ring Road, also known as Boucle de Tahiti, is the busiest road on the island.

It provides picturesque views of the Tahiti Nui main island's coastline, mountains, and lush tropical scenery as it circumnavigates the island. The road has been paved and is normally kept in good condition.

The road across the gorgeous and green Papenoo Valley on the northeastern side of the island is known as the "Papenoo Valley Road."

The route provides spectacular vistas as it travels through forests, crosses rivers, and does so. Check the current conditions before starting this trip since certain parts of this road may be unpaved or bumpy.

On Tahiti's southwest coast, there is a well-known surfing area called Teahupoo. It is possible to go from Papeete in the direction of Teahupoo even if there isn't a set path. Despite certain portions of the route being twisty and tight, the road is typically well-maintained.

On the western side of Tahiti lie the cities of Papeari and Taravao. There are beautiful views of the mountains and the seashore from the route that connects these villages.

Driving on the road is enjoyable due to its pavement and good maintenance.

Please be aware that Tahiti has a generally well-developed road system, particularly in and around its main cities and popular tourist destinations.

There may be fewer lanes or unpaved parts on certain rural or less-used routes. Driving carefully, according to the rules of the road, and being aware of any possible road dangers are always wise decisions.

If you want to hire a vehicle in Tahiti, you should also think about speaking with your rental company about the state of the roads and any particular guidelines or advice they may have.

Tahiti bus routes and bus fares

Both people and tourists like using buses in Tahiti as a form of transportation. A business named "Tahiti Nui Transport," sometimes referred to as "Le Truck," runs the bus system in Tahiti.

The island's principal cities and tourism hotspots are served by these buses on a variety of routes.

In terms of bus fares, they normally vary depending on how far you go. Tahiti is one such place. The prices are, however, subject to change, so it's always a good idea to double-check the most recent prices.

On average, Tahiti bus tickets cost between 200 and 500 Pacific Francs (XPF) for each journey. Shorter travels inside a town or its area may cost between 200 and 300 XPF, while longer routes across the island would cost between 400 and 500 XPF.

These costs are estimates, so they could differ significantly.

It's important to note that getting a "Carte MultiVoyages" (Multi-Journey Card) might save you money. Using the bus often during your stay might make this card more cost-effective since it enables you to pre-purchase a certain number of journeys at a reduced rate.

It is advised to contact the bus company or the local transportation authority as they will have the most recent information available on bus routes, timetables, and rates in Tahiti.

Maps and schedules for buses

The majority of the public transportation in Tahiti, the biggest island in French Polynesia, is made up of buses. A business named "Terevau" runs the bus service on the island.

They provide transportation services to several locations on the island, such as well-liked tourist attractions, neighborhoods, and significant towns.

I suggest contacting local transportation agencies or completing an internet search for the most recent information on bus routes in Tahiti to get the most precise and up-to-date details on bus routes, timetables, rates, and any changes that may have happened after my knowledge cutoff.

Additionally, you can contact the neighborhood tourist information office, which ought to be able to give you the pertinent details.

The Tahiti Ferry System

The biggest island in French Polynesia, Tahiti, is well-known for its breathtaking scenery and clean oceans.

The French Polynesian island of Tahiti does not have a direct ferry link to any other islands, but it does have several ferry services for travel within its island group. A few of Tahiti's main ferry services are listed below:

Papeete, the capital of Tahiti, and Moorea, a neighboring island renowned for its stunning mountains and lagoons, are connected by passenger boats run by Aremiti Ferry. Both standard and high-speed alternatives are available, and the trip lasts around 30 minutes.

Ferry service between Moorea and Tahiti is provided by Terevau. Terevau offers both standard and high-speed ferries for the movement of people and cars, much as Aremiti.

Air Tahiti: This company, which doesn't provide ferries, flies between Tahiti and other French

Polynesian islands on internal routes. For people who want to go more quickly or who are visiting islands that are not immediately accessible by ferries, this is an alternate method of getting between the islands.

It's important to keep in mind that ferry availability and schedules might change, so it's wise to contact individual ferry companies or travel agents for the most recent details on routes, schedules, and ticket costs.

Taxi Services and Costs in Tahiti

Taxi Services: In Tahiti, you can find both official taxi companies and independent taxi operators. Most airports, upscale hotels, and popular tourist destinations provide taxi services.

You may also call a taxi service to request one or ask your hotel to make arrangements for one.

Taxi Cost: In Tahiti, taxi prices are regulated and generally determined by the local government. Distance traveled, the time of day, and any applicable taxes or surcharges all affect the price of a taxi journey. The fact that costs might change makes it vital to have the fare confirmed with the driver before setting off on your trip.

Taxi fare structure: In Tahiti, taxis often use a metering system. The cost of the ride is determined by the distance and length of the trip.

For luggage or late-night journeys, there can be an extra fee. Asking the driver about any possible additional costs can help you prevent unpleasant surprises.

Costs: I am unable to provide exact estimates for Tahitian taxi rates at this time since they may have changed since I had my training, but I can give you a ballpark cost based on what I know now.

Tahiti's base taxi cost as of September 2021 was around XPF 500–600 (about $4.50–USD 5.50), plus an extra fee per mile or per minute of waiting time. Please bear in mind, however, that these numbers may not accurately represent the actual rates.

Advice on Using Taxis in Tahiti

Know how the taxi system works: In Tahiti, taxis are normally identified by a "Taxi" sign on the roof and may be located at approved taxi stands or hailed on the street. Verify the locations of the taxi stands in the places you'll be going.

Confirm availability and negotiate the fare: Since Tahiti does not have a large taxi fleet, it is a good idea to phone and confirm taxi availability in advance, particularly during peak hours or late at night.

It's a good idea to haggle and settle on the fee before getting in the cab to prevent any misunderstandings later.

Even though certain taxis in Tahiti may take credit cards, it is typically safer to carry enough local currency (XPF) to cover your fare in cash.

It's a good idea to have smaller amounts on hand as well since cab drivers may not always have change for bigger ones.

Having the location or destination written down is useful since not all taxi drivers in Tahiti are proficient in English. You may also have the information stored on your phone. By doing this, you can guarantee understanding and avoid uncertainty.

Traffic in Tahiti's metropolitan centers may be crowded, particularly during peak hours, so allow extra time for your trip. Consider this while scheduling your taxi trips, particularly if you have a tour or flight that has to be on time. Add additional time to account for unexpected delays.

Keep valuables with you: Just as when traveling to any other location, it is essential to keep your priceless possessions close to you and avoid leaving them unattended in the cab.

To reduce the chance of theft, stay away from exhibiting pricey jewelry, costly cameras, or huge sums of money.

Be alert of your surroundings: Although Tahiti is usually seen to be secure, it's always vital to be watchful and mindful of your surroundings, especially when taking taxis late at night or in strange places.

Trust your gut, and if you start to feel uneasy, request that the driver pull over somewhere busy and well-lit.

Learn a few fundamental French expressions: Although it's not required, understanding a few fundamental French expressions might be useful when conversing with cab drivers who might not be fluent in English.

A smoother contact will be made possible by simple greetings, numbers, and instructions.

Suitable Ridesharing and Taxi Apps

There are several taxi and ridesharing applications that you may use in Tahiti to make a reservation. Listed below are some suggestions:

TEORIVA: In Tahiti, Teoriva is a well-liked taxi app. It makes it simple and easy for you to get a cab. The app allows you to follow your journey and offers data on the driver and anticipated fee.

UBER: The well-known worldwide ride-hailing service Uber is available in Tahiti. It provides a trustworthy and practical method to schedule a ride with qualified drivers. In addition to upfront pricing, the app also offers cashless payments and driver ratings.

Tahiti's native taxi app is called **_E-TAXI_**. You may reserve a cab in advance or right now. The app offers data about the drivers as well as information on the closest accessible taxis and their anticipated prices.

O-TAXI: O-Taxi is an additional locally owned taxi app that runs in Tahiti. It provides features including simple booking, trip monitoring, and price estimation that are comparable to those of other taxi applications.

When using these apps, make sure to verify their availability in your specific Tahiti location and whether drivers are available at the time and location you specify.

To guarantee a seamless and dependable experience, it's a good idea to compare rates and read reviews from other consumers.

Cycling and Motorcycling Safety Advice and Laws

Prioritizing safety and following local laws are essential while motorcycling and riding in Tahiti. Observe the following guidelines and recommendations:

Wear a Helmet: When biking or riding a motorcycle, always wear a helmet. It's an essential safety precaution that can shield your head in the event of an accident.

Follow Traffic Regulations: Adhere to and abide by all traffic laws. Respecting stop signs, traffic signals, and speed restrictions is part of this.

Keep Yourself Aware at All Times: Be Constantly Alert and Vigilant. Be alert for other cars, pedestrians, and other possible road dangers.

Use Hand Signals: When turning or changing lanes, communicate your intentions by utilizing the appropriate hand signals. By doing this, you may better inform other drivers of your movements.

Keep Away From Other Cars: Keep a safe distance away from other cars, particularly bigger ones. This provides you with ample time to respond and, if necessary, move.

Wear bright or reflective clothing to make yourself more visible to other road users, especially in low-light situations.

Check Your Vehicle: Before you go, check your bike or motorcycle to make sure it is in good operating condition. Check the tires, lights, signals, brakes, and lights.

Avoid Riding While Intoxicated: Never cycle or ride a motorcycle while intoxicated by alcohol or drugs. Your coordination, judgment, and speed of response are all compromised.

Your belongings should be secured by locking them safely if you want to leave your bike or motorcycle unattended to avoid theft.

Get to Know the Local Rules: Learn about Tahiti's unique driving rules and regulations by doing some research. This includes any restrictions on speed, helmet use, or laws that specifically apply to motorcycle and bicycle riders.

Be Aware of the Weather: Pay attention to the weather, particularly during times of rain or storms.

In rainy or slick conditions, reduce your speed and drive more cautiously.

Take Breaks and Stay Hydrated: Long rides may be exhausting, so stop often to relax and replenish your fluids. Your attentiveness and response speed may suffer from fatigue.

Popular Routes for Motorcycling and Cycling in Tahiti

Cycling and motorcycling fans will find magnificent scenery and winding roads on Tahiti, the biggest island in French Polynesia.

While Tahiti doesn't have as many routes specifically designed for cycling as some other locations, the island's breathtaking coastal roads and mountainous terrain make for thrilling rides.

Here are some well-traveled motorbike and bicycle routes in Tahiti:

This well-known route circles Tahiti Nui, the main island, and is known as the Tahiti Nui Loop. You will travel down the coastal route, passing through verdant woods, and quaint towns, and taking in breathtaking ocean vistas, beginning and concluding at the capital city of Papeete. The circle is around 120 kilometers (75 miles) in length.

The starting point for beautiful trips to the well-known surfing location of Teahupo'o is Taravao, which is situated on Tahiti's southwest coast. In addition to valleys, waterfalls, and black sand beaches, the route passes through other attractive natural settings. This route has both difficult mountain parts and seaside areas.

On the east side of Tahiti, in the Papenoo Valley, you may find a more thrilling ride. You go down the Papenoo River, through gushing waterfalls, and extensive jungles.

Although the valley's natural beauty can make the terrain difficult, it is still worth it.

Opunohu Valley: Located on the adjacent island of Moorea, reachable from Tahiti by a quick boat journey, the Opunohu Valley provides a charming ride with breathtaking mountain views.

Both motorbikers and cyclists enjoy the magnificent views offered by the route as it travels past dense jungles, coconut trees, and tiny communities.

Belvedere Lookout: Although there isn't a designated route, Tahitian motorcycle, and cyclist enthusiasts enjoy the journey to the Belvedere Lookout.

Cook's Bay and Opunohu Bay are both visible from the overlook in all directions. The steep, twisting road that leads to the overlook presents bikers with a fun challenge.

Prioritizing safety, donning the proper safety gear, and abiding by local traffic rules is essential before setting off on any motorbike or bicycle journey.

Furthermore, pay attention to the weather, especially during the rainy season when some roads may become more difficult to navigate.

websites for Tahiti transportation

The primary domestic airline in French Polynesia, Air Tahiti, has an official website that may be seen here. It enables you to purchase tickets and offers details about flights, timetables, and prices. the website airtahiti.com

The primary international airport of Tahiti has an official website, Tahiti Faa'a International Airport. It provides details on arrivals, departures, airport amenities, modes of transit to and from the airport, and more. Internet address: www.tahiti-airport.com

Moorea Ferry: For the ferry that travels between Moorea and Tahiti, this website offers information and ticket purchasing options. Schedules, prices, and other pertinent information are included. Internet address: www.mooreaferry.pf

French Polynesia's isolated Marquesas Islands are the destination of one-of-a-kind adventure cruises offered by Aranui Cruises.

On their website, you may get details on itineraries, cruise times, prices, and reservations. the website aranuicruises.com

Tahiti tourist: The official tourist website of Tahiti, provides details on various modes of transportation, including rental vehicles, taxis, and buses, as well as further information on how to get about the islands.

Internet address: www.tahiti-tourisme.com

Tahiti Airport Shuttle: The Faa'a International Airport in Tahiti is accessible through this website's airport transportation services.

To get about the island, they provide both private transportation and shared shuttles. Internet address: www.tahitiairportshuttle.com

Tahiti Nui Travel is a local travel firm that specializes in setting up tours, excursions, and transportation services in Tahiti and the nearby islands.

Their website offers details on various modes of transportation, such as car rentals, transfers, and domestic flights. Visit the website at tahitinuitravel.com.

Le Truck: In Tahiti, Le Truck is a well-liked and reasonably priced mode of public transportation. Even though they may not have an official website, you can get facts about their routes, timetables, and prices by contacting your hotel or visiting the local tourist office.

Moorea Explorer: Moorea Explorer provides transportation between Tahiti and Moorea through boat cruises. On their website, they detail the timetables, costs, and other inter-island transportation services. Moorea Explorer's website

Companies that hire cars: Tahiti is home to several national and international automobile rental agencies.

Even though they may not have dedicated Tahiti websites, you can look for locations and availability in Tahiti on well-known rental car websites like Avis, Hertz, or Europcar.

CHAPTER 6: OPTIONS FOR ACCOMMODATIONS IN TAHITI

Enjoy the perfect Tahitian vacation at our 5-star hotel. Start from $800 per night and lose yourself in the island's magnificence.

Tahiti vacation spots

The biggest and most populous island in French Polynesia, Tahiti has a variety of lovely places to stay. Typical areas to think about are listed below:

The headquarters and largest city of French Polynesia is Papeete, a busy center with a blend of metropolitan conveniences and Tahitian beauty.

It provides a range of lodging choices, commercial areas, markets, and cultural activities.

BORA BORA: Popular with honeymooners and affluent tourists, Bora Bora is known for its recognizable overwater bungalows and breathtaking blue lagoons. It is well-known for its breathtakingly beautiful natural surroundings and bright coral reefs.

MOOREA: Moorea, which is just a short boat journey from Tahiti, is famed for its verdant highlands, spotless beaches, and crystal-clear oceans.

With options for hiking, snorkeling, and dolphin watching, it's the perfect vacation spot for those who love the great outdoors.

HUAHINE: The laid-back, traditional Polynesian vibe permeates this less-visited island. Huahine is well-known for its historical attractions, beautiful bays, and undeveloped beaches
 It's a fantastic option for anybody looking for a more sedate and off-the-beaten-path vacation.

RANGIROA:Rangiroa is an underwater enthusiast's heaven if you're interested in diving or snorkeling. One of the biggest atolls in the world, Tiputa Pass offers exhilarating drift dives and beautiful coral gardens as well as a variety of marine species.

TAHITI ITI: This little island, which is a portion of the larger island of Tahiti, is renowned for its wild beauty and unspoiled scenery. With options for hiking, surfing, and discovering undiscovered waterfalls, it's ideal for nature lovers and thrill seekers.

TETIARO: Marlon Brando used to retire to this private island. It presently houses a prestigious eco-resort with opulent lodging and a stunning natural setting.

Tetiaroa is a remote and picture-perfect location, perfect for a relaxing and sumptuous getaway.

ELEGANT HOTELS

High-end facilities, first-rate service, and a luxurious stay are all provided by luxurious hotels for its visitors.

Numerous variables, such as the location, hotel brand, amenities, and services offered, can affect the price and kinds of opulent hotels. Here are some popular categories of opulent hotels and an idea of their price range:

Luxury City Hotels: These establishments are often found in large cities and include opulent lodgings, fine dining restaurants, spas, and other expensive services.

Depending on the location and the hotel, the price per night might be anywhere from $200 and $800.

Boutique Hotels: Boutique hotels tend to be more compact, individually owned buildings that emphasize giving guests a special and exclusive experience.

They provide posh facilities, individualized service, and modern décor. The cost of a single night might vary from $150 to $600.

Pools, golf courses, spas, and private beaches are just a few of the amenities offered by resort hotels, which are often found in picturesque locations. Depending on the location and amount of luxury offered, the cost each night might range from $250 to over $1,000.

Five-Star Hotels: These are the best-rated accommodations that adhere to the most exacting standards for luxury and service.

They provide first-class facilities, large accommodations, outstanding eating choices, and individualized attention to detail. Depending on the location and reputation of the hotel, rates for five-star lodging may vary from $300 to several thousand dollars per night.

Spa Retreats: Spa retreats put a strong emphasis on well-being and relaxation and provide opulent lodging along with comprehensive spa and wellness amenities.

Depending on the location and degree of luxury, prices might vary from $300 to $1,500 each night.

RESORT

Tahiti has a variety of resorts that can accommodate guests with various needs and budgets. In Tahiti, you may find the following common kinds of resorts:

Luxurious resorts: Private bungalows over the water, immaculate beaches, infinity pools, spa facilities, fine dining options, and individualized services are just a few of the opulent amenities offered by these high-end resorts.

Typically, they offer a variety of pursuits like scuba diving, snorkeling, and cultural excursions.

Compared to luxury resorts, mid-range resorts provide pleasant lodging at more reasonable costs. They might mix rooms with garden or beach views, swimming pools, on-site dining, and entertainment options. Water sports and other activities are accessible at certain mid-range resorts.

Budget Resorts: Tahiti is home to a few reasonably priced resorts that provide simple lodging. Even though these resorts might not have all the luxuries, they still offer a comfortable stay with access to the beach, swimming pools, and other common amenities.

CLAMPING

When compared to resorts, camping is a less popular lodging choice in Tahiti, but the island does have a few camping facilities.

campsites: A few campsites in Tahiti include allocated spaces for campervans or tents. Common amenities offered by these campsites include common cooking areas, restrooms, and showers. They might be found on the island's rich greenery or close to the shore.

Glamping: Glamping, a fusion of luxury and camping, is also possible in Tahiti. Glamping locations provide more luxurious lodging options, including tents with beds and furniture and private toilets. Additional features like on-site dining options, swimming areas, and planned activities are frequently offered.

For reliable information on costs, accessibility, and amenities, it's crucial to do thorough research on certain Tahitian resorts and camping locations.

The most current information is available on their official websites or by getting in touch with them directly.

OVERWATER BUNGALOW

Beautiful overwater bungalows that provide an opulent and attractive lodging choice may be found in Tahiti.

These stilted bungalows provide visitors with an ideal and romantic environment as they are perched above the lagoons' glistening waters.

Overwater bungalows are a feature of several resorts in Tahiti and the nearby islands. Here are a few well-liked examples:

The pinnacle of overwater bungalows is often regarded as Bora Bora. It is home to a large number of opulent resorts that provide a selection of bungalow alternatives, from basic to lavish. The Four Seasons Resort Bora Bora, Conrad Bora Bora Nui, and the St. Regis Bora Bora Resort are a few well-known properties in Bora Bora.

Moorea: Close to Tahiti, Moorea is a stunning island with overwater bungalows. Popular choices include the Hilton Moorea Lagoon Resort & Spa and the Sofitel Moorea Ia Ora Beach Resort.

There are a few overwater bungalows available in Tahiti, an island noted for its colorful culture and beautiful surroundings.

There are two choices on the main island: InterContinental Tahiti Resort & Spa and Tahiti Ia Ora Beach Resort by Sofitel.

Rangiroa: Rangiroa, the second-largest atoll in the world, is well known for having an abundance of marine life. Overwater bungalows are available at the Hotel Kia Ora Resort & Spa in Rangiroa so that visitors may take in the breathtaking lagoon views.

These resorts often have opulent features like private decks, easy access to the sea, glass flooring that allows guests to see below the surface, and sometimes even private pools or jacuzzis. Due to their rarity and great demand, overwater bungalows in Tahiti may cost quite a bit of money.

To ensure availability and to take into account the many packages and services each resort offers, it is advised to make reservations well in advance when making travel plans to Tahiti.

Tahiti also has a tropical climate, therefore it's crucial to choose an occasion that fits your tastes and avoids the rainy season.

Guesthouse And pensions.

For tourists seeking a more personal and genuine experience when visiting Tahiti, guesthouses and pensions are popular lodging alternatives.

Compared to bigger hotels and resorts, these places, which are often managed by local families, provide a more individualized and traditional experience. They are often more intimate and provide an opportunity to engage with the community because of their smaller size.

Think about the following choices to locate guesthouses and pensiones in Tahiti:

Guesthouses and pensioners in Tahiti are often listed on websites like Booking.com, Expedia, or Airbnb.

To aid in your decision-making, you may search for lodging, filter the results based on the kind of hotel, and read reviews left by prior visitors.

Websites for local tourist boards or Tahiti's official tourism department are both good places to start. Typically, these websites offer details on various lodging options, including guesthouses and pensions.

Find guesthouses and pensions by searching web directories that are unique to Tahiti or French Polynesia. Contact information, descriptions, and even reviews may be found in these directories.

Participate in travel discussion forums or read French Polynesia- or Tahiti-focused travel blogs. Travelers often talk about their lodgings, including the guesthouses and pensiones they've been at, and provide suggestions.

Reach out to residents of Tahiti, either natives or ex-pats, through online forums or social media groups. They have personal knowledge of guesthouses and pensiones that may not be well-known and may provide suggestions and insights.

Before booking, don't forget to review the most recent reviews, ratings, and any special conditions or amenities provided by each venue. It's also a good idea to contact the guesthouse or pension directly to check the availability and cost.

Rentals for holidays

Tahiti, a famous vacation spot in French Polynesia, is renowned for its breathtaking scenery, pristine oceans, and opulent resorts. Various elements, including location, amenities, and the season, can affect the cost of vacation rentals in Tahiti.

One of Tahiti's most popular travel spots is Bora Bora, known for its overwater bungalows and azure lagoons. Prices for a modest overwater villa in Bora Bora normally start at around $500 per night.

Vacation rentals on the island may be fairly pricey. However, more opulent lodging can set you back several thousand dollars per night.

Moorea: Moorea is a gorgeous island in French Polynesia that is well-known for its luxuriant highlands, vivid coral reefs, and lovely beaches. On

Moorea, vacation rentals can range in price from budget-friendly lodgings like guesthouses and modest bungalows, which start at about $150 per night, to more upscale beachfront villas and overwater bungalows, which can cost as much as $1,000 per night.

The main island of Tahiti, where the capital city of Papeete is situated, has a selection of vacation rental alternatives.

The location and features of the property might affect the price. On the main island, vacation rentals typically cost between $100 and $300 per night for a small studio or guesthouse and several hundred dollars per night for a bigger villa or beachfront property.

Other islands: French Polynesia is home to several other stunning isles, such as Huahine, Taha'a, and Raiatea.

The cost of vacation rentals on these islands might vary, but generally speaking, they are within the pricing ranges for Moorea and the main island of Tahiti.

It's crucial to keep in mind that these costs are just general ranges and might change widely based on the precise rental property, the season, and any other facilities or services provided. It's often a good idea to check with several vacation rental websites, travel agencies, or neighborhood property management firms to receive precise and current price information for your preferred trip dates.

Tahiti accommodation websites and how to utilize them

You may search for lodging in Tahiti using several different websites. Here are a few well-liked alternatives:

Booking.com (www.booking.com): Booking.com is a well-known website that provides a variety of lodging options, such as hotels, resorts, guesthouses, and vacation rentals.

 input "Tahiti" into the search box on the website, then input your vacation dates and preferences to refine the results.

Airbnb (www.airbnb.com): Airbnb is a well-known website that links visitors with regional hosts who provide a range of lodgings, including individual rooms, complete houses, and distinctive properties.

To use Airbnb, type "Tahiti" into the search field, be sure to include your vacation dates, and then peruse the available properties. The results may be narrowed down using several filters, including price and amenities.

You can book flights, hotels, rental cars, and more via **Expedia (www.expedia.com)**, a comprehensive travel website. Enter "Tahiti" in the search field, choose your trip dates, then explore the list of lodging choices to find a place to stay in Tahiti. The search results may be narrowed down by price, star rating, and property type.

www.hotels.com or hotels.com Tahiti lodging options are many on Hotels.com, which specializes in hotel reservations. To use the website, type "Tahiti" into the search box, then input your vacation dates and go through the list of available hotels.

The results may be filtered by several factors, including cost, guest feedback, and other features.

A confirmation email containing the specifics of your reservation will normally be sent to you once you have made your choice of lodging and finished the online booking procedure. Keep a copy of this email for your records, and be sure to familiarize yourself with the cancellation and refund procedures in case you need to change your reservation.

Here are a few more pointers for efficiently using lodging websites:

Make use of filters: The majority of lodging websites include filters that let you focus your search results based on certain factors like price range, facilities, location, and customer reviews.

To locate lodgings that satisfy your particular needs, use these criteria.

Read reviews: Spend some time reading the opinions of past visitors. They may offer priceless perceptions of the standard of the lodging, the level of service, and the overall journey.

Aspects that are essential to you, such as cleanliness, location, and customer service, may be included in evaluations.

Compare costs; don't stick to just one website. To guarantee you are receiving the greatest bargain, compare prices across several sites.

It is advisable to explore many websites before making a selection since other websites may offer various pricing or specials for the same property.

Direct contact with the property: Consider getting in touch with the property directly if you have any particular queries or unique requests.

Numerous lodging websites offer contact details for the establishment, enabling you to speak with the staff there directly about any issues or demands you may have.

Be wary of extra costs: Bear in mind that certain lodgings could charge extra costs like resort fees or housekeeping fees. Before making a reservation, make sure you are familiar with the property's rules and the total cost of your stay.

When using these websites to book accommodations, be sure to read the property descriptions, and customer reviews, and look up the location on a map to make sure it suits your requirements.

Additionally, to get the best deal, it makes sense to compare prices and offers on various websites.

Once you've located a place to stay that meets your needs, complete the booking process on the associated website by entering the necessary information and paying according to the instructions.

You can identify and reserve appropriate lodging in Tahiti with simplicity if you follow these suggestions and make use of the services offered by lodging websites. Happy travels!

CHAPTER 7: TOP TOURIST ATTRACTIONS IN EACH CITIES IN HAITI AND THE COUNTRY'S FESTIVALS.

Tahiti's Papeete market is a feast for the senses, bringing the warm essence of the Polynesian people to life via regional delicacies and brilliant colors.

Tahiti Heiva I

An important cultural celebration called Heiva I Tahiti takes annually in Tahiti, French Polynesia.

Featuring traditional music, dance, sports, crafts, and other cultural pursuits, it is a vibrant and vivacious celebration of Polynesian culture.

The festival is regarded as one of the most significant and awaited in the area.

During June and July, Heiva I Tahiti typically lasts for several weeks. It brings together competitors from several French Polynesian islands who participate in a variety of categories including handicrafts, music, traditional sports, and dance ensembles.

The traditional dance competition, which features fascinating dances performed by groups from several islands to live music, is the centerpiece of Heiva I Tahiti.

With their sophisticated choreography, vibrant costumes, and indigenous instruments, these dances often depict mythology, history, and everyday life from the Polynesian islands.

Traditional sporting events including outrigger canoe racing, stone lifting, javelin throwing, and coconut tree climbing are included in the celebration along with dancing.

Additionally, there are exhibitions of traditional arts and crafts, such as wood carving, weaving, tattooing, and the creation of traditional attire and accessories, that visitors can take in.

The Polynesian people may present and preserve their rich cultural legacy through Heiva I Tahiti's platform. It draws both residents and visitors who are eager to discover and experience the unique traditions of French Polynesia.

The event acts as a catalyst for cultural dialogue and mutual understanding as well as a source of pride and cohesion for the Polynesian community.

Regatta for Tahiti Pearl

An annual sailing competition is conducted in French Polynesia called the Tahiti Pearl Regatta. It happens in the Society Islands, more especially in the region around Raiatea, Taha'a, and Bora Bora.

The competition is well-known for its stunning tropical scenery, crystal-clear seas, and difficult sailing conditions.

The Tahiti Pearl Regatta regularly draws sailors from all over the globe to the island nation to take part in the competition.

It includes several races spread out over several days, each with a unique set of obstacles and courses.

In addition to traditional Polynesian outrigger canoes, the race is accessible to a variety of sailing craft, including monohulls and multihulls.

The festival highlights competitive racing while also honoring Polynesian culture and the natural beauty of the islands. The chance exists for participants and spectators to get fully immersed in the customs, music, dance, and food of the region.

The regatta often includes cultural performances, beach parties, and other social activities, which makes the whole thing joyous.

The Tahiti Pearl Regatta has established itself as one of the top sailing competitions in the South Pacific.

In it, French Polynesia's unique blend of adventure, competition, and tropical splendor is highlighted. The regatta offers a wonderful experience to everyone engaged, whether they are competitors or spectators.

Marquises Festival

The Festival of the Marquises is a cultural celebration that takes place in the Marquis Islands in French Polynesia.

It values the Marquisians, who are the indigenous population of this area, as well as their art, music, dance, and customs.

Every four years, usually in December, the Festival of the Marquises is held. The opportunity to learn about the distinctive culture of the Marquises draws tourists from all over the world.

Residents of the several islands in the archipelago get together during the festival to showcase their artistic abilities and share their costumes.

Traditional dances, songs, artisan demonstrations, traditional sporting competitions, displays of artwork and handicrafts, and musical performances are among the entertainment options.

The Marquisians now have the chance to share their cultural heritage with the rest of the world and pass it on to the next generations.

Additionally, the festival offers visitors a chance to experience the stunning and well-preserved landscapes of the Marquise Archipelago and get to know its friendly and hospitable residents.

The festival offers conferences, workshops, and trips to further the understanding of Marquise culture in addition to performances and exhibits.

The public is invited to take part in events like making wooden sculptures, making flower crowns, learning traditional dances, and much more.

The Festival of the Marquises is a significant occasion for preserving and advancing Marquise culture. It provides a rare chance to appreciate the fascinating customs, music, dance, and art of these people.

It promises to be an unforgettable experience if you have the opportunity to visit the Marquises during the festival.

Arts Festival in Marquesas

The Marquesas Arts Festival is a cultural celebration of the Marquesas Islands, which are a part of French Polynesia, and its unique arts and traditions.

Music, dancing, carving, tattooing, weaving, and storytelling are just a few of the art forms on display during the festival.

The Marquesas Islands are renowned for their rich cultural heritage and distinctive creative customs. The festival offers a venue for regional creatives to exhibit their works and impart their expertise to locals and tourists from across the globe. It presents a chance to preserve and advance the Marquesas Islands' cultural legacy.

The event offers performances of traditional dances and music, which often include chanting, rhythmic drumming, and complicated motions.

Through exhibits and workshops, local artisans also showcase their skills, showcasing methods like weaving, woodcarving, stone-carving, and tattooing.

The festival often includes storytelling sessions where the history and mythology of the island are recounted, cultural displays, and culinary demos in addition to the arts.

The distinctive practices, rites, and beliefs of the Marquesan people are available for tourists to learn about.

The Marquesas Arts Festival typically lasts for a few days and draws both residents and visitors who want to take in the colorful cultural traditions of the Marquesas Islands.

It gives the Marquesan community a forum for cultural appreciation, celebration, and interaction while also creating a feeling of pride.

Although the Marquesas Arts Festival is a legitimate occasion, specifics may change from year to year.

The best approach to receiving accurate and current information about the event is to study the most recent information and official sources.

"Te Aito"

The phrase "Te Aito" comes from Tahitian Polynesia, notably from the context of the outrigger canoeing sport.

The legendary yearly outrigger canoe race is known as Te Aito is conducted in French Polynesia and is referred to as "the warrior" or "the champion" in Tahitian.

A notable occasion in Polynesian society, the Te Aito race draws competitors from several South Pacific islands.

It displays paddlers' strength, endurance, and ability as they maneuver their canoes through severe ocean conditions. Competitors are striving for the title of Te Aito in the race, which often has both male and female categories.

The racecourse is usually rather lengthy, and competitors must navigate wind, waves, and currents.

It calls for not just strong physical capabilities but Valso familiarity with the water and the ml

To be ready for the competition, participants go through a tough training program that focuses on developing their strength, endurance, and teamwork.

Te Aito has cultural importance in addition to being a race. It promotes the virtues of fortitude, tenacity, and care for the environment while honoring the Polynesian heritage.

Traditional dances, music, and rituals are often included in the competition to commemorate the contestants and their cultural backgrounds.

Te Aito is a prestigious outrigger canoe competition that highlights the athleticism, talent, and cultural pride of Polynesian communities in French Polynesia and beyond.

A material I ni:

A term in the Polynesian language, more especially the Tahitian language, is "material I ni." In English, it means "the Pleiades are high".

A conspicuous star cluster in the night sky, the Pleiades has cultural importance for many Polynesian nations, especially Tahitian culture. Since the Pleiades' position in the sky was historically used by Polynesian cultures for navigation and as a calendar reference, the phrase

"Matari'i I ni'a" is frequently used to denote the beginning of a specific season or time of year.

Kwana Pae:

The phrase "Day of Celebration" or "Festival Day" in English is called "Mahana Pae" in Tahitian. The biggest island in French Polynesia, Tahiti is renowned for its breathtaking natural beauty, colorful festivals, and rich culture.

Tahitians take great pride in their ancestry, and Mahana Pae is a time when people join together to celebrate and present their customs.

Various facets of Tahitian culture, including music, dance, arts and crafts, traditional games, and delectable local cuisine, will be on display during this festival.

Talented dancers often perform during the event, showcasing the fascinating motions of the Tahitian dance known as "Ori Tahiti."

You could also hear or see people performing traditional music and songs using instruments like conch shells, ukuleles, and drums.

In Tahitian tradition, arts and crafts are very significant, and during Mahana Pae, you may find craftsmen showing off their creations.

Intricate wood carvings, woven baskets, tapa fabric, and other classic works of art may be examples of this.

Mahana Pae is no different from any other festival in that food plays a major role. You may enjoy Tahitian cuisine's tastes, which often include fresh seafood, tropical fruits, taro, breadfruit, and coconuts.

Mahana Pae gives residents and tourists the chance to experience Tahitian culture firsthand, as well as to take in exciting performances, sample local cuisine, and experience the kind hospitality of the islanders, even if particular events and activities may change from year to year.

If you're thinking of going to Mahana Pae in Tahiti, it's a good idea to check with the event organizers or the local tourist board for the most recent details on the festival's dates, locations, and activities.

Days Trips in Tahiti

Several day trip choices are available for travelers visiting Tahiti, a beautiful island in French Polynesia. Here are some well-liked day trips you might want to think about while in Tahiti:

Tahiti Iti: Tahiti Iti, sometimes referred to as the "small Tahiti," is the island's smallest peninsula. Compared to the main island, it provides a more isolated and wild experience.

Take a day excursion to Tahiti Iti to explore its lush forests on foot, see secret waterfalls, or just take in the area's unspoiled splendor.

Tahiti Nui, commonly referred to as "big Tahiti," is the bigger region of the island where Papeete, the nation's capital, is situated.

Explore the lively markets in Papeete, go sightseeing at places like the Robert Wan Pearl Museum, or take a scenic drive along the coast to take in the breathtaking scenery.

Known for their vanilla plantations and vibrant Polynesian culture, Taha'a and Raiatea are two nearby islands.

You may go by day to Taha'a and Raiatea to see vanilla fields, find out how vanilla is traditionally made, and get a taste of the local culture.

Tahiti Lagoonarium: The Tahiti Lagoonarium is a unique marine park where you may swim with tropical fish, sharks, and rays in a protected lagoon. It is situated on the northwest coast of Tahiti.

To explore the undersea realm and get up close to the vibrant marine life, you may go on a guided trip or rent snorkeling gear.

Marae Arahurahu: If you have any interest in Polynesian history or culture, you really must visit this place.

Marae Arahurahu is a prehistoric archaeological site with stone platforms and temples that are situated in Tahiti's verdant valleys.

For information on the importance of these holy locations and to obtain an understanding of the island's cultural legacy, take a guided tour.

Papenoo Valley is a charming area on Tahiti's northeastern shore that is perfect for day trips for nature lovers. Cascading waterfalls, tropical woods, and beautiful hiking paths may all be found in this verdant valley.

Explore the valley's natural wonders and take in its breathtaking landscapes by going on a guided hike or renting a 4x4.

Motu Tapu: Just off the shore of Bora Bora sits the little, private islet of Motu Tapu. It is renowned for its immaculate white sand beaches, emerald-colored seas, and breathtaking vistas of Mount Otemanu.

Motu Tapu is a popular destination for day vacations where you may unwind on the beautiful beaches, go swimming in the enticing lagoon, or have a picnic by the beach.

Teahupoo: For thrill-seekers and surfers, a day trip to Teahupoo is an exciting choice. Surfers from all around the globe go to Teahupoo to experience its very large and strong waves.

Even if you're not a surfer, seeing the powerful waves smash onto the reef is breathtaking.

To get closer to the activity and feel the thrill of Teahupoo, you may take a boat trip or hire a native guide.

Arahoho Blowhole: Situated on Tahiti's northeastern shore, the Arahoho Blowhole is a naturally occurring occurrence brought on by the collision of waves with a volcanic tube.

You can see the breathtaking exhibition of water pouring into the air and the blowhole is conveniently located. Keep in mind to maintain a safe distance and use care since the waves might change quickly.

These extra-day travel alternatives provide a variety of experiences, from natural marvels to cultural immersion to heart-pounding activities.

Tahiti is a place that caters to a variety of interests, making sure that everyone may enjoy themselves while there.

CHAPTER 8: FOOD AND RESTAURANTS.

"Food is more than simply fuel; it's a cultural festival, a symphony of tastes that enlivens our palates. Every meal in Tahiti is an invitation toI lj..ob 1 savor the colorful tapestry of Polynesian cuisine, where tropical richness, freshness, and passion combine to create a gastronomic paradise."

Tahiti's regional specialties

The biggest island in French Polynesia, Tahiti, is renowned for its thriving culture and extensive culinary heritage.

Tahiti's traditional cuisine often highlights the region's plethora of fresh fish and tropical fruits. Here are a few of Tahiti's most well-known traditional foods:

Poisson Cru: Also referred to as "Tahitian ceviche," this well-liked meal is created with raw fish that has been marinated in lime juice and coconut milk.

It is often served with fresh herbs and vegetables such as tomatoes, onions, and cucumbers.

Tahitian doughnuts known as **"firi firi"** are prepared with grated taro or cassava, coconut milk, and sugar. Small balls of dough are formed, and they are deep-fried until golden brown.
It is often consumed as a dessert or a snack.

E'ia Ota: E'ia Ota is a delectable raw fish salad prepared in the Tahitian way. Fresh fish, such as tuna or mahi-mahi, is marinated in a mixture of ingredients, including lime juice, coconut milk, onions, tomatoes, and other spices.

The flavors combine to produce a meal that is both acidic and refreshing.

Po'e: A common Tahitian dessert, po'e is created with mashed fruits like banana, papaya, or pumpkin combined with coconut milk, sugar, and sometimes vanilla.

 A sweet and creamy pudding-like dish is the result of steaming or baking the ingredients until it is set.

Ma'a Tahiti: A traditional Tahitian feast that is often prepared for special events or festivals is referred to as ma'am tahiti. Various foods, such as roasted pork, chicken, fish, taro, breadfruit, and sweet potatoes, are frequently served. To provide the cuisine's smokey characteristics, it is customarily cooked in an earth oven called an "umu."

Young taro leaves are cooked with coconut milk and different spices to make the meal known as "fa." It is often offered as a side dish or as an addition to meals with meat or fish.

Poisson Ahimaa is a Tahitian meal that is prepared by marinating fish—typically tuna or reef fish—in lime juice, onions, garlic, and herbs. The fish is then wrapped in banana leaves and baked in a subterranean oven known as an "ahimsa."

The fish acquires a delicate and smokey taste via prolonged cooking.

Breadfruit, also known as **Uluru**, is a common component in Tahitian cooking. This fruit is adaptable and may be cooked, roasted, or fried. Similar to potatoes, it is often served as a starchy side dish with savory foods.

Roast pork is the main ingredient in the well-known Tahitian meal known as **Pua'a Roti**.

A fragrant mixture of herbs, spices, and sometimes soy sauce or coconut milk is used to marinade the pork. It is then slowly roasted until it is soft, and rice or taro is given as a side dish.

Tahitian tamales are called pahi, a typical delicacy from that country. It is prepared by wrapping banana leaves over a combination of shredded taro, coconut milk, and sometimes fish or meat.

The wrapped bundles are then steam-cooked, producing a meal that is flavorful and filling.

Ti'o (Taro Pudding): Made from taro, coconut milk, sugar, and sometimes vanilla, Ti'o is a delicious treat. After being boiled until tender, the taro is mashed or pureed.

The mixture is sweetened and made thicker to produce a creamy, delectable treat that resembles pudding.

Meals to Come Across In The City

Tahiti's hallmark dish, poisson cru, is a must-try. It includes raw fish that has been marinated in coconut milk and lime juice, along with veggies including tomatoes, cucumbers, and onions.

Poulet Fafa is a well-known Tahitian meal that is made with chicken, taro leaves, coconut milk, onions, and spices.

Ecrevisses à la Tahitienne: Freshwater crayfish are cooked in mouthwatering coconut milk, lime juice, ginger, garlic, and spice sauce in this meal.

Ma'a Tahiti is the name for a customary Tahitian feast that often consists of a range of foods. It often includes fish, coconut milk-based sauces, taro root, breadfruit, roasted pig (pua), and tropical fruits.

Sashimi: Because Tahiti is so close to the water, it is simple to get fresh, high-quality fish there. You may have sashimi, which is raw fish that has been finely sliced and is sometimes accompanied by soy sauce, wasabi, and pickled ginger.

Mahi-Mahi is a well-liked fish in the South Pacific. It is often grilled and served with a tasty marinade or a side of tropical fruit salsa.

Poisson à la Vanille: Tahitian vanilla is well-known around the globe and is used in a variety of cuisines. In a meal known as poison à la vanille, fish, such as red snapper, is cooked in a sauce that has been flavor-infused with vanilla.

Freshly made coconut bread is a popular dessert in Tahiti. It is prepared using coconut milk, shredded coconut, and sometimes vanilla or other seasonings. Eat it as a snack or for breakfast.

Chao Men: Tahiti's version of fried noodles is called chaos men. Typically, it consists of stir-fried noodles with mixed veggies, your choice of meat or fish, and Tahitian seasonings.

Despite not being a uniquely Tahitian dish, many restaurants in Tahiti serve delectable steak frites, which consist of grilled steak served with a side of crunchy French fries.

Tahitian bread called pharaoh is produced from breadfruit that has been roasted and crushed. It is often eaten as a snack or with meals and has a distinctive flavor and texture.

Using fermented fish or shellfish, lime juice, onions, and different spices, fanfare is a traditional Tahitian condiment. It is used to give food a tangy, savory taste.

Tahiti is renowned for the profusion of exotic fruits on its fruit platter. A fruit tray with pineapple, mango, papaya, bananas, passion fruits, and other tasty treats is available.

I'a Ota: Made with fresh fish, lime juice, coconut milk, chopped veggies, and seasonings, I'a Ota is a Tahitian dish in the manner of ceviche. It delivers a delicious fusion of creamy and citrus tastes.

Pahi: The term "pahi" refers to a fish stew prepared in the Tahitian manner, which includes a variety of shellfish, coconut milk, tomatoes, onions, garlic, and flavorful herbs. It is a filling and cozy meal.

Pua'a Roti: Pua'a Roti is a typical Tahitian meal that consists of slow-cooked, spice-marinated, roasted pork. It often comes with veggies and a tasty sauce on the side.

Bananas of the Fe'i kind are native to French Polynesia. It is often served as a side dish or dessert and is roasted or steamed. It's a delicious treat because of its sweet and creamy texture.

Tahitian Vanilla Ice Cream: Tahiti is well-known for its vanilla, so you may have creamy, fragrant Tahitian vanilla ice cream that highlights the island's distinctive taste.

Fafa de Taro: Taro leaves are cooked in coconut milk and spiced with onions, garlic, and herbs to make this classic Tahitian cuisine. It is often included as a side dish with entrees.

Tahitian Raw Fish Salad: This salad includes raw fish that has been marinated in lime juice, coconut milk, and different spices, similar to Poisson Cru. It is served with a vibrant mix of vegetables to create a meal that is light and refreshing.

Coconut Curry is one dish in Tahitian cuisine that combines ingredients from several cultures. It blends a mixture of spices with the smoothness of coconut milk and may include vegetables, poultry, or seafood in it.

Traditional Tahitian cuisine called Pape Ena is created with grated and roasted breadfruit combined with coconut milk, vanilla, and sugar. It is often prepared as a sweet treat and cooked till golden.

Chicken stew made in the Tahitian manner with tomatoes, onions, garlic, and spices is known as poulet fricassé. It is often eaten with rice or with classic side dishes like taro or breadfruit.

Tahiti's Seafood Prices And Variety

Tuna (Thon): Fresh, frozen, or canned tuna are all readily accessible in Tahiti and are very well-liked there. The cost per kilogram might vary from 1,500 to 3,000 XPF depending on the tuna's kind and grade.

Mahi-Mahi (also known as dorado) is another common fish in Tahitian cooking. It has a moderate taste and a solid texture. Fresh Mahi-Mahi may cost between 1,500 and 2,500 XPF per kilogram.

Red Snapper (Vivaneau): Red Snapper is a tasty fish that is eaten often in Tahiti. It tastes delicately sweet and delicious. Fresh Red Snapper may cost anywhere between 2,000 and 3,500 XPF per kilogram.

Lobster (Langouste): In Tahiti, lobster is considered a premium seafood dish. Depending on their size and availability, the cost of live lobsters might vary significantly. For fresh lobster, budget between 8,000 and 15,000 XPF per kilogram.

Shrimp (Crevette): Shrimp may range in price based on size and quality, and it is commonly accessible in Tahiti. The cost per kilogram normally varies from 2,000 to 4,000 XPF.

Octopus (Pieuvre): A common seafood dish in Tahitian cuisine is an octopus. Fresh octopus may cost between 2,000 and 4,000 XPF per kilogram.

Prawns (Crevette): Prawns are a bigger species of shrimp with a somewhat distinct taste. They often appear in a variety of seafood cuisines. In Tahiti, fresh prawns may cost between 3,000 and 5,000 XPF per kilogram.

Popular fish known for its meaty texture and mild flavor is the **swordfish (Espadon).** Fresh swordfish might cost anywhere between 2,500 and 4,000 XPF per kilogram.

Crab (Crabe): Crabs, which come in a variety of sizes and species, are a popular ingredient in Tahitian cuisine. Depending on the variety and size, fresh crabs may cost anywhere between 4,000 and 8,000 XPF per kilogram.

Mussels (Moules): A favorite among seafood enthusiasts, mussels are often used in seafood stews. Fresh mussels may cost between 1,500 and 3,000 XPF per kilogram.

Clams (Palourde): Several Tahitian seafood recipes include clams, another kind of shellfish. Fresh clams might cost anywhere between 2,000 and 4,000 XPF per kilogram.

It's crucial to remember that seasonality and regional market circumstances may affect both the availability and cost of seafood. It's recommended to check with seafood merchants in Tahiti or visit local markets to receive the most up-to-date information.

TAHITI SEAFOOD VENDORS

The Papeete Market (Le Marché de Papeete) is a lively marketplace that sells a variety of regional goods, including fresh seafood, in the nation's capital city.

There are several vendors offering fish, crabs, shrimp, and other seafood products.

Both residents and visitors use there often to purchase fresh fish, shellfish, and other seafood goods.

Restaurants on the Waterfront: Tahiti has several waterfront eateries, many of which focus on serving fish. These places often provide the freshest fish of the day that has been cooked in regional or foreign methods. You may relish mouthwatering seafood while taking in stunning ocean views.

Local fishermen may be seen selling their catch directly since Tahiti has a rich fishing tradition. It's worthwhile to investigate coastal regions or seek advice from locals on where to locate fishermen selling seafood.

Le Marché de Papeete, or the "Fish Market of Papeete," is a bustling marketplace selling regional foods, particularly seafood.

Local Supermarkets and Grocery Shops: Fresh fish is often stocked at Tahiti's many supermarkets and grocery shops. You may discover a variety of seafood alternatives in Tahiti's two main grocery brands, Carrefour and Super U.

Restaurants & Food Stalls: Tahiti is well-known for its mouthwatering seafood dishes, and the island is home to a large number of seafood-focused restaurants and food stands. You could discover restaurants that specialize in seafood by exploring coastal areas, especially those that are close to well-known tourist attractions.

Local suggestions: Asking for suggestions from locals is one of the finest ways to find undiscovered treasures and real seafood experiences. The employees at your hotel, your tour guides, or other nice locals you encounter may often provide advice on the top seafood shops or eateries in the neighborhood.

Expensive Food And Restaurant Rates

Fine Dining Restaurants:

$15 to $40 for an appetizer.
Entree: $40 to $100
a dessert: $15–$30

Michelin-Star Restaurants:
The cost of the tasting menu ranges from $150 to $500 per person.

$50 to $150 for a dish at a restaurant that serves only meals from a certain chef.

Beginning/Appetizer: $20–$60
$50 to $150 for a meal.

Desserts: $20 to $40

It's crucial to remember that these costs are just broad estimates and may vary widely based on the venue, it is standing, and the menu items themselves.

Taxes, service fees, and gratuities are furthermore often excluded from the above-mentioned pricing.

Exceptional service, a distinctive setting, and well-chosen wine or drink pairings are often included in upscale dining experiences in addition to the meal itself.

 For the most precise and recent information on their menu selections and pricing, it is advised to visit the particular restaurant's website or get in touch with them directly.

Depending on the variety and uniqueness, wine costs might vary significantly.
Ten to thirty dollars for a glass of wine.

$50 to $500 or more for a bottle of wine (and considerably more for rare or vintage wines).

Menus from the Chef:

These menus, which are often created by the chef, provide a specially crafted gastronomic experience. Depending on the restaurant and the quantity of meals offered, prices per person might vary from $100 to $500 or more.

Packages for fine dining:

A whole dining experience is included in certain high-end restaurants' all-inclusive packages.

A welcome drink, many dishes, wine pairings, and other benefits may be included in these packages. These packages range in price from $200 per person to several thousand dollars, depending on the restaurant and degree of exclusivity.

It should be noted that owing to their popularity and limited seating options, fine dining experiences sometimes need reservations in advance.

It's also a good idea to verify the restaurant's standards before going since dress regulations could be enforced in certain posh venues.

Personal dining areas:

For special events or private meetings, several opulent restaurants provide private dining rooms.

The size of the space, the menu, and any other services offered may all have a significant impact on the cost of private dining rooms.

Depending on the restaurant and desired degree of opulence, prices might go from a few hundred dollars to several thousand.

gastronomic experiences

Gourmet experiences that are exclusive to high-end restaurants include chef's table eating and kitchen tours.

These experiences provide a more personal and intimate view of the cooking process, hence prices may be higher than those for standard eating alternatives.

Gourmet experiences may cost anything from a few hundred and over a thousand dollars per person.

Luxury Add-Ons: To improve the eating experience, upscale restaurants often provide extra services and facilities in addition to the food itself.

These could include attentive waitstaff, sommelier services, and customized menus.

Every city in Tahiti has a street food vendor.

French Polynesia's biggest island, Tahiti, is renowned for its breathtaking scenery, exciting culture, and mouthwatering food.

Even though there might not be as many street food vendors in Tahiti as in some other places, you can still find local treats to satiate your palate.

Here are some well-liked Tahitian street food options to try:

Roulottes: In Papeete, the capital of Tahiti, roulottes—food trucks or food stands—come to life in the evenings. These lively food trucks, which are close to the ocean, provide a range of dishes, including French, Chinese, Tahitian, and more.

There are many different foods available, including crepes, grilled meats, seafood, poisson cru (a raw fish salad from Tahiti), and delectable regional sweets.

Snack Bars: Snack bars are a kind of modest, unpretentious restaurant located all across Tahiti. These nearby eateries are well-liked by the neighborhood since they provide fast and inexpensive meals.

You can eat sandwiches, fried noodles, grilled fish, plate lunches (with rice, pork, and veggies), poisson cru, and grilled fish.

While exploring the island, keep an eye out for signs that read "Snack" or "Snack Bar".

Tropical fruits are abundant in Tahiti, which is fortunate. Bananas, pineapples, mangoes, papayas, coconuts, and other freshly selected fruits are available at fruit stands and tiny market booths.

These stalls often sell fruit smoothies and drinks that are produced using fresh local ingredients.

Street vendors may be seen offering regional delicacies or treats, albeit they are not as common as in some other places.

Look for vendors selling coconut bread, coconut candy, fire (deep-fried pastries that resemble doughnuts), po'e (a classic Tahitian delicacy made from bananas and breadfruit), and po'e.

Tahiti's prices and beverage options

French Polynesia's biggest island, Tahiti, has a wide selection of cool, tropical beverages that are well-liked by both natives and tourists. You may find the following sorts or variations of beverages in Tahiti:

In French Polynesia, which includes Tahiti, Hinano Beer is a well-known regional beer brand. Both residents and visitors often drink this light beer since it is so refreshing, particularly on the beach or during social events.

Mai Tai: Rum, orange liqueur, lime juice, and sometimes a dash of grenadine or other fruit juices are the main ingredients in this well-known Polynesian drink.

It is a typically offered tropical and fruity beverage at Tahitian bars and resorts.

Papeete Punch is called after the city, which serves as the capital of French Polynesia. A tasty and energizing beverage is often produced by blending rum or vodka with a variety of tropical fruit juices, including pineapple, orange, and passionfruit.

Fresh coconut water is widely available in Tahiti because of the island nation's profusion of coconut palms. It is a healthy, hydrating beverage that is often consumed alone or combined with other fruits to make delectable smoothies.

Noni Juice: The tropical fruit noni, which grows in Tahiti, is renowned for its health advantages. For its conceivable medical benefits, noni juice is created by extracting the juice from the noni fruit.

Pineapple Juice: Pineapples are a common crop in Tahiti, and freshly squeezed pineapple juice is a favorite option for a cool beverage. It may be consumed by itself or combined with other fruit juices to make tasty concoctions.

Vanilla Tea: Tahiti is renowned for its premium vanilla, and vanilla tea is a calming and fragrant beverage produced by infusing hot water with vanilla pods or extracts. The nuances of Tahitian vanilla may be enjoyed in this manner.

The Fenua Colada is a Tahitian variation on the traditional Pia Colada that blends regional ingredients including coconut cream, pineapple juice, and often a dash of local rum. It's a smooth, tropical drink that's ideal for soaking up the island spirit.

TAHITI RESTAURANT WEBSITE

The website for Le Coco Restaurant is a well-known restaurant in Tahiti. The menu, a calendar of events and activities, and contact details are all included in this website's information on the eatery.

Along with a map of the neighborhood, the website also features images of the restaurant and its food. Additionally, the website allows users to reserve a table online. **https://www.lecocorestaurant.com/**

Le Maitai Polynesia Resort's website is another well-liked Tahitian restaurant website. This website provides details about the resort's activities, features, and services.

A map of the region and pictures of the resort are also available on the website. The website also enables online booking for rooms and suites. https://www.lemaitai.com/

The website for the Le Meridien Tahiti Resort is the third popular restaurant website in Tahiti. On this website, you may learn about the resort's features, services, and activities.

A map of the region and pictures of the resort are also available on the website.

The website also enables online booking for rooms and suites. https://www.lemeridientahiti.com/

Le Lotus Bleu, online at www.lelotusbleu.pf

The website for La Villa Mahana is lavillamahana.pf

Visit Le Tahaa at www.letahaa.pf.

Visit La Plage at www.laplagetahiti.com.

Le Coco Beach may be found at www.cocobeach.com.

www.labaliene-restaurant.pf, La Baliene Restaurant

Visit La Plage de Robinson online at **www.laplagederobinson.com**.

Visit Le Cottage at **www.lecottage.pf**.

La Maison de la Mer, available online at **lamaisondelamer.pf**

La Veranda is located at **laverandatahiti.com**.

CHAPTER 9: LANGUAGE AND CURRENCY

Tahiti's national tongue

The Tahitian language is widely used in Tahiti. Austronesian in origin, Tahitian is connected to other Polynesian languages including Hawaiian, Maori, and Samoan.

In French Polynesia, which includes Tahiti, it is the most extensively used native tongue. French, which is the official language of French Polynesia, is also frequently used and worth mentioning.

French and Tahitian are both widely spoken languages in Tahiti.

Every city speaks a different language.

French Polynesia's Tahiti island is the biggest and most populated. As French Polynesia is an overseas collectivity of France, French is the primary language used throughout the region, including Tahiti. Tahiti is a cosmopolitan country, hence there are other languages spoken there as well.

Some of the languages you could hear in Tahiti's several cities include the following:

Papeete is the largest metropolitan area on the island of Tahiti and the capital of French Polynesia. Tahitian is another language that many people in the area speak in addition to French.

French and Tahitian, a Polynesian language, are both recognized as official languages.

On the island of Tahiti, southwest of Papeete is the commune of Faa'a. Similar to Papeete, the two main languages spoken in Faa'a are French and Tahitian.

Close to Faa'a on Tahiti's west coast lies another commune called Punaauia. In Punaauia, people often speak French and Tahitian.

Mahina: On Tahiti's northeastern shore, there is a commune called Mahina. French and Tahitian are the two primary languages used here.

On Tahiti's northwest coast, not far from Papeete, lies the commune of Pirae. Tahitian and French are the two main languages used in Pirae.

Papara: The commune of Papara is situated on Tahiti's southwest coast. The two most often used languages in Papara are French and Tahitian.

USEFUL TAHITIAN PHRASE TO KNOW

"Ia ora na" is a typical Tahitian salutation that translates to "hello" or "good day." It's an appropriate method to welcome natives and show respect for their culture.
Here are some other useful words that may be useful to you while you are there:

"Mauruuru" is a Tahitian term that means "thank you." When a local helps you out or does a service, it's usually polite to thank them.

In Tahitian, "Nana" is the word for "goodbye" or "see you later." It's a cordial method to wish a person you've gotten to know throughout your stay goodbye.

The Tahitian phrase "para," which means "I don't understand," may be used to indicate that you don't know the language or can't speak it.

Locals will respect your attempt at communication and may switch to a language you are more used to.

When asked, "Eaha te huru?" - This word's translation is "What is the price?" It might be useful to ask about the price of an item while negotiating or purchasing at a neighborhood market or store.

"Aita" - This term may be used to reject an offer or to indicate "no." It's a straightforward method to convey your lack of interest or desire.

The question "Eaha te paari ra?" The meaning of this phrase is "Where is the beach?" This query might assist you in finding your route if you're trying to find the closest beach.

"Aroha nui" is a phrase that translates to "much love" or "lots of love." It's a cozy and kind approach to show someone you appreciate or care for them.

When dining in Tahiti, the phrase "Tama'a maitai" can be used to express "bon appétit" or "enjoy your meal." It's a nice approach to wish other people a delicious supper.

"Muruuru roa" is a term that may be used to convey extreme gratitude or admiration and meaning "thank you very much." It is an expanded form of "Mauruuru" and expresses a greater degree of gratitude.

"Ehia te ora?" - This question has the answer "What time is it?" This query is helpful if you want to arrange your activities or find out the time.

The question "E haere au i te fenua?" I'm going sightseeing, as this line is translated. Use it to indicate that you want to explore the island and all it has to offer.

"E para hi ta'u moni, murumuru" – If you need to trade money, it means "I would like to exchange money, please." It may be useful when dealing with regional banks or money exchange businesses.

What do you mean by "Teie te mau here?" These lyrics ask, "Are these the traditional songs?" You may use this expression to enquire about the kind of songs being played if you're taking in a cultural performance or enjoying local music.

"Te Aroha ia oe" translates to "I love you." It's a sincere sign of devotion and love. Use it with extreme care, and only when necessary.

The question "E aha te nui o te para?" - This query is code for "How much is the ticket?" This phrase can help you ask about the cost while buying tickets for an event or transportation.

Remember that communicating in the local language and learning a few simple words may improve your trip by demonstrating respect for Tahitian culture. Even if your pronunciation isn't great, the locals will still be grateful for your attempt.

The System of Tahitian Money

Currency Symbol: The CFP Franc's symbol is ",", which is similar to the French Franc's. To prevent confusion with the outdated French Franc, it is most often written as "XPF".

Exchange Rate: Because of its connection to France, the CFP Franc has a set exchange rate with the Euro (EUR). 1 EUR equals 119.33 XPF at the fixed rate. The CFP Franc's value is thus linked to the value of the Euro.

Coins and Notes: The CFP Franc may be found as a coin or a note. Coins come in 1, 2, 5, 10, 20, 50, and 100 Franc denominations. 500, 1,000, 5,000, and 10,000 Franc banknotes are among the denominations available.

The images and patterns on the coins and banknotes are meant to symbolize the rich cultural history and scenic beauty of Tahiti and other French Pacific possessions.

Acceptance: In Tahiti, the CFP Franc is the sole accepted form of payment for all commercial transactions, including travel, eating, and lodging. But in tourist hotspots and larger establishments, major credit cards and foreign debit cards are also frequently accepted.

Exchange and Availability: Tahiti offers banks, currency exchange services, and ATMs as places to get CFP Francs. In metropolitan regions and popular tourist locations, ATMs are widely accessible.

Additionally, some companies might accept foreign currencies like the US dollar or euro, but it is best to have local currency on hand for day-to-day transactions.

The Banque de France is the central bank in charge of managing the CFP Franc's issuance and circulation. In collaboration with the French government, it regulates monetary policy and currency stability.

It's important to keep in mind that while Tahiti utilizes the CFP Franc as its official currency, certain bigger resorts and establishments that cater to tourists could also list pricing in US Dollars owing to the presence of visitors from other countries. However, for local transactions, the CFP Franc continues to be the dominant currency.

Cash Handling And Reporting Requirements

The French Pacific Franc (CFP franc), sometimes known as the XPF, is Tahiti's official currency. In several French overseas territories, including French Polynesia, which includes Tahiti, the CFP franc is in use.

Banknotes and coins both exist for the CFP franc. 500, 1,000, 5,000, and 10,000 XPF banknotes are the most prevalent ones in use. There are 1, 2, 5, 10, 20, 50, and 100 XPF coins available.

Reporting and Cash Handling Requirements

Financial institutions, companies, and people may be compelled to disclose cash transactions that exceed certain levels. Local laws or regulations may establish these thresholds, which vary depending on the jurisdiction.

Customer Due Diligence (CDD): Financial institutions are usually obliged to do customer due diligence, which involves confirming the client's identification and determining the goal and nature of the commercial connection.

This procedure assists in identifying and reducing the dangers connected to money laundering and other illegal actions.

Financial institutions and other reporting organizations are often required to disclose any transactions or conduct that gives rise to suspicions of money laundering, supporting terrorism, or other illegal activity.

Record-keeping: Companies can be obliged to keep track of all cash transactions, including information on the sums involved, the dates involved, and the people involved. According to local legislation, these documents must be kept for a certain amount of time.

cash Reporting: while the quantity of cash or negotiable instruments a person is carrying exceeds a predetermined limit, they may be obliged to disclose it while entering or departing a nation. Usually, customs officials are in charge of enforcing this rule.

CHAPTER 10: CLUBS AND NIGHTLIFE IN TAHITI

In Tahiti, the clubs serve as the paintbrushes used to paint the sky with the hues of music, laughing, and unadulterated joy.

Overview of the Entertainment Scene in Tahiti

Step into the pulsating rhythm of Tahiti's nightlife, where the clubs are alive with pulsating beats, and the air is filled with the contagious energy of the South Pacific.

From sunset to sunrise, the dance floors of Tahiti's clubs beckon you to give in to the intoxicating melodies and let your body sway to the hypnotic music. In the heart of this paradise, where the warmth of the island embraces you, the nightlife of Tahit

French Polynesia's biggest island, Tahiti, is recognized for its breathtaking natural beauty, crystal-clear oceans, and lively culture.

Even though Tahiti is perhaps best known for being a paradise in the tropics, it also has a vibrant and diverse entertainment scene. An overview of Tahiti's entertainment scene is provided below:

Traditional Polynesian Dance: Tahitian dance is an essential component of the community's culture and something that tourists should not miss.

"Ori Tahiti" dance performances are characterized by dynamic movements, colorful costumes, and thumping drum sounds. These performances often take place at festivals, special events, and at resorts and cultural institutions.

Tahiti commemorates its illustrious musical legacy via several festivals and events. Local artists combine modern elements with traditional Polynesian instruments like the ukulele and the pahu (Tahitian drum).

The biggest cultural event in Tahiti, Heiva, is a yearly festival that features music concerts, traditional sports, and dance contests.

evening: The French Polynesia city of Papeete, which is situated on the island of Tahiti, has a vibrant evening scene.

You may enjoy local and foreign music, dancing, and entertainment at a variety of taverns, clubs, and live music venues. The "Roulettes," or seaside promenade, is a well-liked meeting place for both residents and visitors, providing a lively environment with food trucks, live music, and street entertainment.

Cultural institutions: Tahiti is home to several cultural institutions where you may learn more about the local performing arts and entertainment scene.

The Papeete Maison de la Culture presents exhibits, theatrical productions, concerts, and dance events that highlight the skills of regional artists. To encourage traditional arts and crafts, the center regularly hosts seminars and events.

Outdoor Recreation: Tahiti's natural setting provides a wealth of outdoor amusement options. There are many things you may partake in, from hiking to water sports.

Popular water sports include snorkeling, scuba diving, surfing, and boating, while hiking paths let you explore lush mountains, waterfalls, and picturesque vistas.

Casinos: Tahiti offers a few casinos where you may test your luck at different games including blackjack, poker, and slot machines if you're looking for a little excitement. To enhance the gaming experience, these casinos often organize live entertainment activities and performances.

Excursions & Cruises: Many tourists visiting Tahiti choose to go on organized tours or cruises, which often include onboard entertainment like live music concerts, Polynesian dance performances, and cultural displays. You may have fun while taking in the beauty of the islands thanks to these adventures.

Tahiti's nightlife has been influenced by its culture.

The biggest island in French Polynesia, Tahiti, is renowned for its breathtaking natural beauty, welcoming people, and dynamic culture.

Tahiti's nightlife is shaped by a combination of French and other global influences, as well as the traditions and practices of the Polynesian people.

Following are some significant cultural influences on Tahiti's nightlife:

Polynesian Traditions: Music, dancing, and storytelling are highly valued in the Polynesian culture. Tahitian nightlife often puts a focus on the rapid drum beats of the "tenure" and the elegant hip motions of the "one's," among other traditional Polynesian music and dance. Hotels, restaurants, and special entertainment Venus

French Influence: Tahiti has incorporated aspects of French culture into its daily life as a result of being a French overseas possession.

In restaurants and bars, French cuisine, wine, and Champagne are frequently ordered. Many businesses combine French and Polynesian design elements to produce distinctive ambiance and menu options.

Live Music and Performances: Local bands and artists often provide live music to spice up Tahitian nightlife. These performances include a range of musical genres, from modern Pacific pop, reggae, and jazz to traditional Polynesian tunes.

A few locations also feature traditional entertainment like fire knife demonstrations and cultural events with dancers.

Heiva Festival: Held every year in Tahiti, the Heiva Festival is a notable cultural occasion. Through music, dance, sporting events, and traditional crafts, it honors Polynesian culture and is held in June and July.

Both residents and tourists attend the event, which fosters a lively environment and a flurry of nighttime activities.

Beach Bars and Resorts: The breathtaking beaches of Tahiti provide the ideal setting for beach bars and resorts. These places often provide a relaxed setting where customers may unwind, sip tropical drinks, and take in stunning surroundings.

After dark, a festive ambiance is created by the live music that some beach bars play.

Traditional Food: Tahitian food contributes to the nightlife scene as well. Local eateries and food stands often sell traditional fare including roast pig, taro-based treats, and poisson cru (raw fish cured in coconut milk and lime juice).

A cultural and gastronomic trip in and of itself may be had by trying these unique foods.

Cultural Centers and Events: Throughout the year, Tahiti's cultural centers, such as the Maison de la Culture in Papeete, hold a variety of events, exhibits, and performances.

Through cultural immersion, these events give attendees the chance to experience Tahitian arts, crafts, music, and dance, enriching the nightlife scene.

Popular Tahiti nightclubs

Le Roof Nightclub is a well-liked hangout for both residents and visitors in Papeete, the capital of Tahiti. With live music, DJs, and a dance floor that looks out over the ocean, it provides a lively scene.

Soirée Club Tahiti: Soirée Club Tahiti is a popular nightlife destination located in Punaauia. It plays a variety of musical styles and often holds themed gatherings and special occasions.

La Casa Mahina is a hip nightclub that is well-liked by locals. It is situated in the commune of Mahina on Tahiti's northeastern coast. It boasts a large dance floor with a variety of music styles, including Latin, EDM, and regional songs.

Le Retro Dancing is a nightclub that blends vintage aesthetics with contemporary music. It is located in Faaa, a village close to Papeete. It draws a broad clientele and often presents live entertainment and theme evenings.

Pink Coconut: A well-known nightclub in Tahiti, Pink Coconut is located in Papeete. It has a fun environment and a variety of musical styles, including both national and local songs. Additionally, it regularly hosts live performances by DJs.

Beachfront Lounges and Bars

Le Coco's is a chic seaside pub and club in Punaauia that is renowned for its laid-back vibe and stunning views. They provide a selection of beverages, such as cocktails, beers, and wines. Locals and visitors alike enjoy visiting it.

Le Sunset is a beachside bar with a combination of lounge chairs and bean bags directly on the sand. It is located on the west coast of Tahiti. It's a fantastic location for relaxing, unwinding, and taking in the sunset across the sea.

Le Mayflower is a seaside bar in Tahiti's capital city of Papeete. It boasts a relaxed atmosphere and serves a variety of beverages, such as tropical cocktails and regional beers.

Both residents and visitors seeking a laid-back seaside atmosphere frequent Le Mayflower.

Le Carre is a beachfront pub and nightclub on Lafayette Beach that is renowned for its energetic ambiance and live music.

It provides a selection of beverages and often holds gatherings and parties. It's a fantastic location for mingling and taking in the coastal atmosphere.

Le Belvédère is a beachside pub and club with sweeping views of the lagoon that is situated in Faa'a. It's a well-liked location for unwinding and drinking around dusk.

They provide a selection of drinks, such as mocktails and cocktails.

Live Music Locations

Theatro is a well-known nightclub in Papeete that often presents live music performances by both local and foreign musicians. It has a lively atmosphere and a range of musical styles.

Le Royal Kikiriri is a popular bar and nightclub in Papeete that features live music performances from regional bands and DJs. It features a variety of musical genres and is a well-liked hangout for both residents and visitors.

Le Piano Bar is a quiet establishment where you may listen to live piano music and sometimes live performances by local artists. It is situated in downtown Papeete. It provides music lovers with a calm and private atmosphere.

Les 3 Brasseurs: Les 3 Brasseurs is a brewery in Papeete that sometimes hosts live music. In addition to serving a variety of specialty brews, it offers a relaxed and welcoming setting for taking in live performances.

The Yellow Lounge is a restaurant and bar in Punaauia that periodically features live music performances by bands and acoustic artists. It provides a relaxed ambiance along with a selection of cuisine and beverages.

Remember to confirm the most recent details on these locations, their timetables, and any entrance requirements before making travel arrangements.

Cultural and traditional performances

French Polynesia's biggest island, Tahiti, is renowned for its rich cultural legacy and traditional performances. Here are a few well-known Tahitian cultural performances and traditional shows:

Heiva Festival: Usually celebrated in July, the Heiva Festival is Tahiti's most important cultural celebration.

Through a variety of traditional performances, including music, dance, and sporting events, it celebrates Polynesian culture. It's a wonderful chance to see genuine Tahitian handicrafts, crafts, and traditional attire, as well as traditional games like va'a (outrigger canoe) racing.

Tamure: Tamure is a Tahitian traditional dance that is distinguished by quick hip motions, elegant hand gestures, and vivid costumes. Men and women both perform it, and it often has upbeat drumming and singing in the background.

Tamure dance performances may be seen in hotels, cultural institutions, and on special occasions.

Otea Dance: Otea is a strong and vivacious dance form that has its roots in Tahiti. It includes chanting, coordinated motions, and rhythmic drumming. Male and female dancers move their hips and feet quickly and expressively.

Aparima Dance: Aparima is a slower, more lyrical dance form that uses expressive hand motions and beautiful hand gestures to convey tales. It often illustrates myths, love tales, or natural phenomena. You may see a prima dance performance at cultural gatherings, lodgings, and traditional performances.

The Fire Knife Dance is a common element of cultural events and demonstrations, despite not being indigenous to Tahiti. Although it has been incorporated into Tahitian entertainment, it is Samoan in origin.

A knife with a blazing blade is twirled and maneuvered by expert dancers, producing a fascinating show of light and motion.

Visits to Maraes: Maraes are revered locations where people congregate for religious rites and cultural celebrations. A visit to a marae allows you to learn about the cultural and historical importance of these hallowed locations, while it is not a performance in the traditional sense.

You may find out about traditional Polynesian practices and customs at certain maraes via guided tours or cultural shows.

Unusual Nighttime Activities

Tahiti is a great place to go stargazing because of its pristine sky and low levels of light pollution. Visit a remote beach or sign up for a stargazing tour to take in the magnificent night sky.

Constellations, shooting stars, and even the Milky Way may be seen.

Nighttime Kayaking: Take a nighttime kayaking adventure to see Tahiti's stunning lagoons as they are illuminated by the moon. Watch the bioluminescent plankton as you paddle through the calm water as they produce a breathtaking natural light display by illuminating the water all around you.

Traditional Tahitian Dance Shows: In the evening, take in a traditional Tahitian dance performance to learn more about the rich Polynesian culture.

These performances give a comprehensive cultural experience while showcasing the vivid costumes, bouncy music, and captivating dances of Tahiti.

Sunset Dinner Cruises: Take a charming dinner cruise as the sun sets off the shore of Tahiti. Sail aboard an opulent yacht or a classic outrigger canoe, and enjoy a sumptuous meal while you watch the sunset over the horizon.

It's the ideal way to unwind and take in Tahiti's breathtaking splendor at dusk.

Fire dance: Attend a beach party or a cultural event to see the mesmerizing art of fire dance. A visually breathtaking sight is created when talented performers display their ability by whirling and manipulating burning items while performing hypnotic fire dances.

Explore Tahiti's bustling night markets, such as the Papeete Market, which come to life after sundown. These markets provide a huge selection of regional handicrafts, trinkets, fresh fruit, and delectable street cuisine.

It's a wonderful chance to get immersed in the community's culture and meet the welcoming Tahitians.

Restaurant and Food Suggestions

Traditional Polynesian cuisines and foreign influences coexist in Tahiti. For your trip to Tahiti, consider these dining and cuisine suggestions:

If you visit Tahiti, you must try the island's signature dish, poisson cru. It comprises raw fish blended with veggies and marinated in lime juice and coconut milk, then served with breadfruit or taro.

In a lot of neighborhood eateries and food stands, you can find delectable Poisson Cru variations.

Roulottes: These are food trucks that travel and congregate around the shore in Papeete, particularly at night. Chinese, French, and Tahitian cuisines are among the many options available at roulottes.

In a lively and relaxed setting, it's a great place to sample a variety of foods like grilled fish, crepes, chow mein, and more.

La Plage de Maui is a beachfront restaurant with spectacular ocean views and a laid-back ambiance that can be found on Tahiti's west coast.

They provide a variety of meals from across the world and Polynesia, as well as fresh seafood, grilled meats, and tropical drinks. For a leisurely lunch or supper, it's the perfect location.

Le Coco's: Le Coco's is a well-liked eatery in Papeete that serves French-inspired food with a Polynesian twist.

A variety of culinary items are available, including foie gras, steak tartare, and local seafood specialties. The restaurant offers a lovely garden setting and a pleasant atmosphere.

Le Lotus is an elegant restaurant that provides outstanding fine dining experiences. It is housed inside the InterContinental Tahiti Resort & Spa.

The restaurant offers sweeping views of the lagoon since it is built on a platform above the water. Tahitian lobster and grilled tuna are just a few of the meals on their menu that combine French and Polynesian tastes.

Les Roulottes de Vai'ete is a bustling food market in the heart of Papeete that's a wonderful place to sample regional cuisine. There are several food carts there serving a variety of cuisines, such as Chinese, Tahitian, and French.

You may choose from a variety of delicacies, such as grilled seafood and BBQ meats, to tropical sweets, to satiate your appetites.

Snack Mahana is a well-liked alternative if you're searching for a relaxed and reasonably priced meal option.

This neighborhood restaurant is located in Punaauia and offers traditional Polynesian fare such as grilled fish, poisson cru, and taro preparations. It's a fantastic location to sample traditional Tahitian cuisine.

CHAPTER 11: BEACHES AND MUSEUMS IN TAHIT.

The coasts are the scene of "Nature's masterpiece, where the melody of waves meets the warmth of golden sand. Tahiti's beaches are said to be a haven of peace where anxieties may slowly go and dreams might emerge.

BEACHWEAR ETIQUETTE AND DRESS CODE

Beachwear Manners:

Swimwear: Swimwear, such as swimsuits, bikinis, or swim trunks, is often suitable while at the beach or pool.

Cover-ups: It's a smart idea to have a cover-up, sarong, or beach dress on hand to wear while you aren't in the water. Particularly while leaving the beach or pool areas, this might assist preserve modesty and demonstrate respect for the local culture.

respecting regional traditions Be cautious of the regional traditions and laws while visiting a beach in a foreign nation. Particularly in religious or traditional settings, it may be customary to wear more modest swimwear.

Beach club or resort attire:

Check the exact requirements: Certain resorts or beach clubs may have dress standards for their facilities, requiring visitors to wear appropriate footwear, shirts, or cover-ups while entering restaurants, bars, or other interior areas, for example.

Casual vacation attire Shorts, T-shirts, sundresses, and sandals are often appropriate casual wear for beach resort environments.

Avoid overexposure: Although beachwear is appropriate in most outdoor areas of a resort or beach club, it's still necessary to preserve some modesty and stay away from garb that is too provocative or insulting.

Events or Beach Parties:

Theme-specific attire: If you're going to a beach party or other event with a certain theme, be sure to dress according to the rules. Costumes, tropical designs, or particular hues could be included.

Wear loose clothing: Choose comfortable outdoor-appropriate apparel, such as summery casual attire, light materials, shorts, and sundresses.

Pack layers: Consider packing a lightweight sweater or jacket to keep oneself warm as temperatures may drop even at the beach in the evenings or on breezy days.

Public Beaches

Respect local laws: Various publicly accessible beaches may have their standards for conduct and attire. To guarantee that you are being courteous, familiarize yourself with any stated rules or regional traditions.

Good judgment and modesty: It's typically advisable to act modestly and abstain from wearing unpleasant or extremely exposing apparel, even at public beaches.

Think about cultural sensitivities: If you're in a foreign nation, be mindful of the local cultural norms and sensibilities. More conservative attire may be expected or even needed in certain locations, particularly in those with a strong religious presence.

Tahiti's famous beaches

Tahiti, a French Polynesian island, is renowned for its stunning beaches and beautiful oceans. Here are a few well-known beaches in Tahiti:

Near the community of Paea, on Tahiti's southern coast, is the stunning white-sand beach known as **Plage de Maui**. Swimming, snorkeling, and picnics are all popular activities there.

Plage de Toaroto: Plage de Toaroto is a stunning black sand beach with calm waves that can be found near Punaauia on Tahiti's western coast. It's a terrific location for unwinding, tanning, and watching beautiful sunsets.

Plage de Taharuu: Popular with surfers because of its strong waves, Plage de Taharuu is a beach on Tahiti's southeast coast near Papara. The dense flora that envelops the shore enhances its natural attractiveness.

Plage Lafayette: Plage Lafayette, located near Arue on Tahiti's northeastern coast, provides a stunning location with fine black sand and crystal-clear turquoise seas. Swimming and snorkeling are both highly recommended here.

Plage de Vaiava: This quiet beach in Punaauia, next to the InterContinental Tahiti Resort, is renowned for its calm seas and stunning coral reef. It's a great location for snorkeling and seeing the diverse aquatic life.

Pointe Venus Beach: Located near Mahina on Tahiti's northern shore, Pointe Venus Beach is a well-liked vacation spot for both residents and visitors.

It is a wonderful location for swimming and tanning since it has a charming lighthouse and a mixture of rocky and black sand regions.

Hidden Gems: Lesser-known Beaches in Tahiti

Tahiti is well known for its magnificent beaches and outstanding natural beauty. While some beaches on the island are well-liked by tourists, other hidden gems provide a more private and serene experience. You may want to check out the following undiscovered beaches in Tahiti:

Plage de Maui: With its immaculate white sand and turquoise waves, Plage de Maui, which sits on Tahiti's east coast, is a hidden treasure. Swimming, snorkeling, and sunbathing are all excellent activities there.

You can appreciate the peace and natural beauty of the region since the beach is often calm and less crowded.

Plage du Taharuu: Located on Tahiti's southern coast, this lovely black sand beach is well-known for its exceptional surfing conditions. Compared to other well-liked surfing locations, it is a local favorite and attracts fewer visitors.

If you don't surf, you may still take in the breathtaking environment and unwind on the volcanic beaches.

Plage de Vaiava: This beach provides a tranquil and calm ambiance and is situated on Tahiti's western coast. A lovely location for leisure surrounds the beach with lush flora and palm palms.

Picnics, shoreline strolls, and sunset viewing are all excellent activities there.

Plage de Mitirapa is a secluded cove with white beaches and brilliantly blue seas that is located on the southeast coast of Tahiti.

For those looking for a quiet escape, this isolated beach provides seclusion and calm. With vibrant coral reefs and exotic creatures to see, the beach is also renowned for its exceptional snorkeling options.

Plage de Tiarei: This undiscovered treasure on Tahiti's northeastern coast is renowned for its picturesque scenery and quiet waves.

Beautiful views of the coastline may be seen from the beach, which is bordered by green mountains. Swimming, kayaking, or just relaxing on the soft sands are all great activities to enjoy there.

Tahiti's water sports and beach activities

The biggest island in French Polynesia, Tahiti, is well known for its beautiful beaches, clean seas, and variety of water sports and activities. You may enjoy the following popular water sports and beach activities in Tahiti:

Snorkeling and diving are popular activities in Tahiti because of the island nation's gorgeous coral reefs.

Exploring the underwater world through diving and snorkeling is highly recommended. There are coral gardens to explore, tropical fish to swim with, and even sea turtles, sharks, and rays to see.

Tahiti is a popular surfing destination because of its strong waves that might be difficult to ride. On the island's southern shore lies a surf break known as Teahupo'o, one of the biggest and most magnificent in the world.

Surfers of all levels converge here for spectacular barrels and huge rides.

Stand-up Due to Tahiti's calm lagoons and gentle waves, stand-up paddleboarding (SUP) has become increasingly popular.

You may maneuver through calm seas while paddleboarding, explore the shoreline, and take in breathtaking island vistas.

Renting a jet ski and riding across Tahiti's crystal-clear seas is an amazing experience.

Speeding through lagoons, finding undiscovered coves, and experiencing the rush of skimming over the waves are all possibilities.

Yachting & Sailing: The beautiful seas that surround Tahiti are ideal for yachting and sailing. A sailing trip may be had by renting a boat and visiting nearby islands, secret harbors, and serene lagoons.

Kayaking: Paddle slowly along Tahiti's coastline or across its tranquil lagoons. Discovering undiscovered beaches, viewing marine life, and taking in natural beauty can all be done in a tranquil and enjoyable manner this way.

Fishing in the deep water is fantastic off the coast of Tahiti. Attempt your luck at catching marlin, yellowfin tuna, mahi-mahi, and other game fish by joining a fishing charter. For fishing fans, it's an exhilarating experience.

Parasailing: Experience Tahiti's magnificent vistas from above via parachute.

A boat will raise you far above the sea while pulling a parachute that is fastened to you. Enjoy the sweeping views of the sea and the nearby islands.

Whale watching: If you go to Tahiti between July and November, you will have the opportunity to see the spectacular humpback whales as they migrate yearly.

Experience a boat tour to see these magnificent animals breaching and having fun in the water.

Beach soccer and volleyball courts may be found on several Tahiti beaches. To have some sun-filled pleasure, gather your pals or participate in a nearby activity.

TAHITI MUSEUMS

The Museum of Tahiti and the Islands is situated close to Papeete, the capital of Tahiti, in Punaauia. Through exhibits, artifacts, and educational displays, it highlights the history, culture, and natural heritage of French Polynesia.

The Gauguin Museum, which is located in Papeari, is devoted to preserving the legacy of the famous French painter Paul Gauguin. His paintings, sketches, and sculptures are on display in the museum.

James Norman Hall Museum: Honoring American writer and aviator James Norman Hall, the James Norman Hall Museum is situated in Arue.

Manuscripts, personal effects, and artifacts about Hall's life and his South Pacific adventures are on display at the museum.

The black pearl's importance in French Polynesia is examined at the Museum of Tahiti Black Pearl, which is located in Punaauia.

Visitors may understand the cultural significance of this gem while learning about the pearl business and seeing magnificent pearl jewelry.

Robert Wan Pearl Museum: Located in Papeete, this museum is devoted to the world of pearls in general and the Tahitian pearl in particular.

The museum features a spectacular collection of pearl jewelry as well as information on the history, science, and workmanship of pearl production.

French Polynesia's rich plant variety is shown at the Papeari Museum known as the Museum of Tahiti's Gardens. It has sizable gardens filled with different plant species, including indigenous and medicinal ones, as well as displays of traditional Polynesian agriculture and horticulture.

The watercolor paintings of the Museum of Tahiti's Watercolors, which is located in Punaauia, were created by both local and foreign painters and were inspired by the local wildlife, people, and way of life. It presents an original viewpoint on the area's creative past.

The Museum of History and Ethnography of Papeete, which is situated there, offers information on the customs, history, and culture of Tahiti and the other islands. It has displays of conventional crafts, antique pictures, and items from antiquity.

Museum of Tahiti Tattoo and Arts: Located in Punaauia, this museum honors the tradition of tattooing, which is deeply ingrained in Tahitian culture.

Through exhibits, live demonstrations, and engaging displays, visitors can learn about the background, symbolism, and tattooing methods of the Tahitian people.

The Papeari-based Museum of Prisons provides a unique viewpoint on French Polynesia's history of criminal justice. It exhibits the former jail buildings, together with the cells, tools of torture, and old records, giving information about the local judicial system.

The Maraa Grotto Interpretation Center is a resource for information and displays on Tahiti's Maraa Grotto. It is situated in Paea. The grotto's geological structure, cultural value, and flora and fauna may all be discovered by visitors.

Beach Safety Advice for Tahitians

Prioritizing your safety is crucial while visiting Tahiti's beaches. The following vital advice will help you have a safe and pleasurable beach experience:

Examine the weather: Always look at the weather prediction before going to the beach. Going to the beach during a storm or when bad weather is predicted is not recommended since it might be harmful.

Swim only in specified areas: Seek out beaches with lifeguards and only swim there. Usually, flags or markers are used to designate these places. In the event of an emergency, lifeguards are taught to keep an eye on the state of the water.

Tahiti's seas may have powerful currents, especially around reef breaks, therefore use caution while swimming in them. When entering the water, pay attention to any warning signs and proceed with caution.

To escape a current's draw if you find yourself trapped in one, consider swimming parallel to the coast.

Apply waterproof sunscreen with a high SPF rating on your skin to protect it from the intense tropical sun. Apply it again frequently, particularly after swimming or perspiring.

Remain hydrated because Tahiti's hot and muggy weather can make you dehydrated. If you want to spend a lot of time at the beach, make sure you drink lots of water to keep hydrated.

The varied marine life and stunning coral reefs of Tahiti are well-known worldwide. Coral is delicate and easily destroyed, so avoid touching or stomping on it. Keep your distance from marine life and refrain from feeding or bothering it.

The majority of the marine life in Tahiti is safe, but it's always a good idea to remain on the lookout for them. Avoid touching any jellyfish or other stinging creatures you come across, and if a lifeguard is on duty, alert them. If stung, get medical help right away.

Respect your limitations: Recognize your swimming limitations and remain in your comfort zone. Consider donning a life jacket or utilizing other flotation devices if you lack strength in the water.

Children must always be properly supervised while at the beach, so take extra precautions. Always keep an eye on them, even for only a few whiles, and make sure they remain in shallow water.

Maintaining awareness of your surroundings will help you avoid any potential dangers. Watch out for sharp coral, submerged rocks, and any sudden changes in the depth of the water.

Please keep in mind that the goal of these suggestions is to increase your safety when you visit Tahiti's beaches. Always abide by local laws and ordinances, and heed the guidance of lifeguards or other beach officials.

CHAPTER 12: TIPS FOR A MEMORABLE TAHITIAN VACATION

Hidden Gems and Must-See Attractions

Tahiti's Jardin Botanique de Papeari is a botanical garden with a varied array of tropical plants and flowers. It is situated in the hills.

Visit the tranquil surroundings and learn about the local flora by taking a guided tour.

Point Venus is a historically noteworthy location where Captain James Cook saw the transit of Venus in 1769. It is located on Tahiti's northern shore.

Visit the lighthouse, take in the stunning coastal scenery, and explore the black sand beach.

Faarumai Waterfalls: The Faarumai Waterfalls are a magnificent setting with several waterfalls surrounded by tropical foliage, hidden away in Tahiti's lush valleys. You may see the waterfalls' unadulterated splendor from a variety of vantage points reached by hiking routes.

Les Trois Cascades, which translates to "The Three Waterfalls," is another stunning waterfall location in Tahiti. This well-kept secret has a trio of lovely waterfalls, and you may cool down in the pools underneath them.

Tahiti Iti, the tiny portion of Tahiti, is a jewel just waiting to be discovered but is sometimes overlooked by its bigger cousin.

It provides a calmer and more off-the-beaten-path experience thanks to its beautiful beaches, gorgeous walks, and laid-back vibe.

Arahoho Blowhole: Situated on Tahiti's northeastern shore, the Arahoho Blowhole is a naturally occurring phenomenon wherein waves smash into a constrained lava tube, producing an amazing show of water spouts.

On the island of Tahiti, there is a serene oasis called Vaipahi Gardens, which has lush foliage, colorful flowers, and calm strolling routes. Enjoy this hidden gem's tranquility by taking a leisurely walk.

Visit Taharaa Viewpoint for spectacular panoramic views of Papeete and the mountains in the area. It provides a wonderful view, particularly at dawn and sunset.

The Museum of Tahiti and Her Islands is a great place to go if you want to learn more about Tahiti's extensive cultural legacy. Polynesian history, art, and customs are shown at the museum.

Tips for Traveling on a Budget

You don't have to forgo the quality of your trip just because you're traveling on a tight budget.

You may have an unforgettable vacation while keeping your costs in control with some careful preparation and wise decisions.

Some suggestions for traveling on a tight budget are as follows:

Create a budget for your vacation and do much study as you begin to plan and prepare. Look for locations, modes of transportation, and lodgings that are within your budget.

Websites and forums for traveling might provide insightful advice from other travelers.

Off-peak travel is recommended since costs for lodging, transportation, and attractions are often cheaper.

If you want to take advantage of cheaper travel, think about going at off-peak times or when there are fewer tourists. Fewer people will be around, and you'll have a more genuine local experience.

Use online travel comparison tools to locate the cheapest costs: tools like Skyscanner, Kayak, and Booking.com let you compare prices from various flights and hotels.

Use the "flexible dates" or "search nearby airports" choices to uncover more affordable alternatives, and be flexible with your trip dates.

Consider staying in a cheap hotel: Look for inexpensive lodging choices like hostels, guesthouses, or cheap hotels. Alternative lodging choices, which are often less expensive than conventional hotels, include Couchsurfing and Airbnb.

Cooking your food or eating where the locals do might save you money. Consider staying in a place with a kitchen so you can prepare part of your meals to save money.

This enables you to enjoy affordable meals while seeing neighborhood markets and grocery shops. To save money while dining out, try to find neighborhood restaurants or street food vendors.

Take the bus or walk: Public transit is often less expensive than a cab or a rented vehicle. Plan your plans after doing some research on the local public transit choices.

Another excellent method to see a city and save money on transportation is to walk about.

Give free or inexpensive attractions a priority. Many places provide these attractions, which are also excellent cultural experiences. Visit local markets, festivals, parks, and museums with free or reduced admission days.

To discover more about the city, take advantage of free walking tours, historical landmarks, and nature trails.

Travel in groups or look for travel companions: Traveling in groups can help you save money by dividing costs for lodging, transportation, and other expenses.

To split costs and meet new acquaintances along the journey, you may also discover travel companions via internet forums or platforms.

Pay attention to your spending: Track your outgoings daily and adhere to your spending plan. Avoid impulsive purchases and place more value on experiences than possessions.

Use budgeting tools or a trip notebook to monitor your spending and remain on target.

Be adaptable and willing to consider other options since sometimes traveling presents unanticipated chances. Keep an open mind and be willing to consider last-minute deals, itinerary changes, or alternate routes.

You may uncover cost-saving options and maximize your budget by being adaptive.

Always prioritize experiences above amenities while traveling on a tight budget. You can enjoy a fantastic vacation without going overboard if you prepare in advance, do your homework, and keep an eye on your spending.

PHOTOGRAPHIC ADVICE AND THE TOP INSTAGRAM LOCATIONS

Tahiti, which is renowned for its spectacular natural beauty and immaculate beaches, provides a wealth of options for beautiful photography and Instagram-worthy locations.

Whether you're a seasoned photographer or an avid Instagram user, here are some pointers and the finest locations in Tahiti for taking stunning pictures:

Photos of the sunrise and sunset

Moorea: For breathtaking dawn views across the mountains, go to Belvedere Lookout or Opunohu Bay.
Visit Venus Point or Teahupoo in Tahiti Iti to see a beautiful ocean sunset.
Overwater Villas:

Bora Bora: Photograph the recognizable overwater bungalows against the emerald-colored water and Mount Otemanu's background.

Book a stay at a Tahiti resort with overwater bungalows, like Le Meridien Tahiti or InterContinental Tahiti Resort, and take photos of the colorful sunsets from your private deck.

Waterfalls:

The majestic Fautaua Waterfall, which is close to Papeete, is situated in a gorgeous environment surrounded by luxuriant vegetation.

Explore the pathways in Vaipahi Gardens to find secret waterfalls that provide interesting picture possibilities.

White Sand Beaches:

Venus Point: This beach provides a spectacular contrast for your images because of its reputation for having black sand and historical importance.

Taharuu Beach, a black sand beach on Tahiti's southern coast, is a great place to take photos of the spectacular coastline.
Island: Motus

Taha'a: Take photographs of the island's pristine seas, palm palms, and white sand beaches by exploring the Motus that surrounds it.

Take a day trip to Tetiaroa to capture images of its quiet beaches, abundant marine life, and magnificent landscape.

Experiences with Culture:

Visit the Papeete Market to take photos of the brightly colored vegetables, ethnic crafts, and local goods.

Marae Arahurahu: This historic temple complex provides a glimpse into Tahitian culture and a striking setting for photographs.

Photographing underwater:

Moorea: While scuba diving or snorkeling in the lagoons, discover the coral gardens and abundant marine life.

Rangiroa: This atoll, which is renowned for its top-notch diving locations, presents chances to photograph aquatic marvels including dolphins, sharks, and vibrant fish.

Photo Advice:

Golden Hour: To capture beautiful images, take advantage of the warm, mellow light during dawn and dusk.

Rule of Thirds: Use the rule of thirds to compose your photographs, positioning important objects along the fictitious gridlines to create greater balance and visual appeal.

Use water surfaces, such as lagoons or swimming pools, to reflect gorgeous patterns in your photographs.

Consider using a wide-angle lens to capture the vast surroundings and make your subject stand out against them.

Try Different viewpoints: To add diversity to your compositions, try taking photos from various viewpoints, such as low angles or bird's eye views.

When taking pictures of people, especially in more private situations, always be mindful of the local culture and request their consent.

Create wonderful memories of this island paradise while enjoying your Tahiti photography adventure!

SHOPPING AND SOUVENIRS RECOMMENDATIONS

Tahiti is well-known for its stunning black pearls, which are grown in the emerald-colored lagoons that surround the island.

There are various shops and pearl farms where you may buy a variety of pearl jewelry, such as necklaces, earrings, and bracelets.

Tifaifai Quilts: Tifaifai quilts are hand-stitched traditional Tahitian quilts. They have vivid colors and elaborate motifs that often show the local flora and animals. These quilts are lovely and genuine mementos.

Monoi Oil: Coconut oil is infused with Tiare flowers to create monoi oil, a Tahitian beauty product. It is used on the skin, hair, and body for massage.

Look for bottles of Monoi oil at neighborhood stores or go to a factory to learn more about the manufacturing process.

Woodcarvings: Polynesian gods are shown intricately and symbolically in Tahitian woodcarvings, sometimes referred to as tiki carvings.

Try to find miniature tiki sculptures, masks, and other wooden items handcrafted by regional craftspeople.

Pareos: Pareos are vibrant, thin textiles that look great as scarves, dresses, skirts, and beach wraps. They come in many different patterns and styles, often with tropical themes or conventional Polynesian prints.

Tahiti is renowned for its premium vanilla products. In regional stores and markets, you can find vanilla beans, vanilla-infused goods like extracts and sugar, as well as lotions and candles with a vanilla scent.

Paintings, sculptures, ceramics, and woven baskets are just a few examples of the lively and varied local art produced in Tahiti.

Look for art markets and galleries where you can find one-of-a-kind works produced by regional artists.

Crafts made locally: Tahitian crafts include things like shell necklaces, woven baskets, headgear, and vintage musical instruments like ukuleles and drums.

These unique gifts are crafted by hand and showcase the rich Polynesian culture.

Remember that negotiating is not expected while purchasing in Tahiti. In contrast to tourist districts, you may often discover greater deals in local markets.

Additionally, make sure you are informed of any customs rules or limitations of the export of specific goods, such as black pearls or wood carvings, to your home country.

Enjoy your time spent shopping in Tahiti and bring home trinkets that will serve as a lasting reminder of the islands' natural beauty and rich culture.

Practices for Sustainable Travel

Choose environmentally friendly lodgings: Look for hotels, resorts, or lodges with green certifications or sustainable practices in place, such as using renewable energy, saving water, and putting waste management techniques into effect.

Reduce carbon footprint: Whenever possible, use low-emissions transportation options like using trains or buses instead of flying.

If you must travel, think about reducing your carbon footprint by aiding initiatives that cut down on greenhouse gas emissions.

Support the local economy by traveling responsibly and purchasing from and supporting regional companies, artists, and communities.

Eat at neighborhood eateries, get gifts from nearby markets, and employ neighborhood tour guides. This helps to distribute tourism revenue more evenly and contributes to the local economy.

Respect local culture and traditions: Learn about and respect the customs, traditions, and beliefs of the places you visit. Dress appropriately, be mindful of local customs, and follow cultural norms. Engage in activities that promote cultural exchange and understanding.

Conserve natural resources: Be conscious of your water and energy usage while traveling. Take shorter showers, reuse towels and bed linen, and turn off lights and electronics when not in use. Respect natural habitats, wildlife, and protected areas by following designated paths and refraining from littering.

Minimize waste: Reduce waste generation by carrying a reusable water bottle, shopping bag, and food container. Avoid single-use plastics and dispose of waste responsibly by using designated recycling and composting facilities.

Support conservation initiatives: Contribute to conservation efforts by participating in eco-friendly activities such as wildlife conservation projects, nature walks, or volunteering opportunities. This helps to protect fragile ecosystems and biodiversity.

Choose responsible tour operators: Select tour operators or travel agencies that prioritize sustainable practices and adhere to ethical guidelines. Look for certifications like Global

Sustainable Tourism Council (GSTC) accreditation, which ensures the operator's commitment to sustainability.

Educate yourself and others: Learn about the local environment, culture, and history of the places you visit. Share your knowledge and experiences with others to raise awareness about sustainable travel practices and encourage more responsible behavior

Choose locally sourced and organic food: Support sustainable food practices by seeking out restaurants and eateries that serve locally sourced, organic, and seasonal food.

This reduces the carbon footprint associated with food transportation and supports local farmers and producers.

Engage in responsible wildlife tourism: When encountering wildlife, prioritize their well-being and conservation. Avoid activities that exploit or harm animals, such as riding elephants, swimming with captive dolphins, or visiting venues that promote animal performances.

Instead, choose wildlife encounters that focus on observation, education, and conservation efforts.

Participate in community-based tourism: Look for opportunities to engage with local communities through community-based tourism initiatives.

This can involve homestays, cultural exchanges, or activities that provide direct economic benefits to the community while respecting their cultural integrity and way of life.

Use sustainable transportation options at your destination: Once you arrive at your destination, choose sustainable transportation methods such as walking, biking, or using public transportation to explore the area.

This reduces reliance on private vehicles and helps to minimize congestion and air pollution.

Practice responsible diving and snorkeling: If you enjoy underwater activities, choose dive operators that adhere to sustainable diving practices.

Respect coral reefs and marine life by not touching or damaging them, and avoid purchasing souvenirs made from endangered species or coral.

Support conservation organizations: Consider donating to local or international conservation organizations that work to protect natural and cultural heritage. These organizations often engage in research, habitat restoration, and community development projects that promote sustainable tourism.

Leave no trace: Practice the "leave no trace" principle by leaving natural areas, historical sites, and public spaces as you found them. Dispose of waste properly, refrain from taking natural souvenirs, and avoid damaging or disturbing fragile ecosystems.

Offset your travel impact: Calculate your travel-related carbon emissions and consider purchasing carbon offsets. Carbon offsets support projects that reduce greenhouse gas emissions, such as renewable energy initiatives or reforestation programs.

CHAPTER 13: WATER SPORTS AND RECREATION

Snorkeling and Scuba Diving

Scuba diving in Tahiti:

Popular Snorkeling Locations: Tahiti has several locations that are well-known for snorkeling, including Moorea Lagoon, Tahiti Iti, Matira Beach near Bora Bora, and the atolls of Rangiroa and Ragiroa.

Marine Life: Tahiti offers a great range of marine life for snorkelers to see, including vibrant coral formations, tropical fish species, sea turtles, rays, and even dolphins.

Accessibility: Tahiti offers a variety of snorkeling locations that are simple to reach by land or sea, making them suitable for both novice and seasoned snorkelers.

Hotels, diving shops, and trip organizers often provide snorkeling gear for hire.

To dive underwater in Tahiti:

Dive Sites: Tahiti has a wide range of superb dive sites that can accommodate divers of all levels of experience. Particularly well-known diving locations include those in the vicinity of Tahiti, Moorea, and Bora Bora.

Popular selections include places like Moorea's Aquarium, Tetopa, and the Taapuna Pass.

Coral reefs and marine life: While diving in Tahiti, you may discover vibrant coral reefs alive with a variety of marine life, such as reef fish, sharks, manta rays, eagle rays, and sometimes even humpback whales during the seasonal migration.

The visibility in Tahiti's seas, which ranges from 60 to 100 feet (18 to 30 meters), is normally acceptable for diving. Between 79°F (26°C) and 84°F (29°C), the water's average temperature is consistently warm throughout the year.

According to the location and the tide, currents might change, therefore it's best to ask local dive operators for more information.

Certification & Dive Operators: If you're not a trained scuba diver, Tahiti provides possibilities for novices to obtain certification via dive courses offered by approved dive operators.

The greatest diving locations may be found with the help of several knowledgeable dive operators who can also guarantee safety and fun.

surf and kiteboarding

Tahiti is renowned for its top-notch surf breakers, including the recognizable Teahupo'o. Tahiti is a popular destination for surfing. Professional surfers go from all around the world to ride the enormous, strong waves at Teahupo'o.

Teahupo'o is a really difficult wave, nevertheless, and is recommended for advanced surfers only, it's crucial to remember. Tahiti still boasts a lot of other surf places that deliver waves that are more forgiving whether you're a novice or intermediate surfer. Papara, Papeeno, and Taapuna are a few well-known surf spots in Tahiti.

May through September are the finest months for surfing in Tahiti because the waves are bigger and more constant throughout this season.

Tahiti is a great place to kiteboard because of the ideal winds and waves. A perfect setting for this thrilling water activity is provided by the lagoons and trade winds.

Due to its consistent winds and picturesque lagoons, Moorea, an island close to Tahiti, is especially well-known for kiteboarding. Known for their flat water and consistent winds, Moorea's Opunohu Bay and Haapiti are excellent places to go kiteboarding.

Lagoons in Tahiti Iti, Vairao, and Fa'a' are a few other locations for kiteboarding. The austral winter (May to October), when the trade winds are strongest, is the ideal season for kiteboarding in Tahiti.

Safety and Precautions: When kiteboarding or surfing in Tahiti, it's crucial to put safety first. Consider these crucial safety measures:

Recognize your level of expertise and choose kiteboarding and surf breaks that are appropriate for you.

Ensure safe conditions for your chosen activity by checking the weather and wave reports before leaving the house.

Respect local laws and customs, and be considerate of other kiteboarders and surfers. Be aware of any applicable laws and customs. Avoid snatching other people's waves by being aware of the queue order.

Apply the right tools: Check to see whether your kiteboarding or surfboard is in excellent shape and appropriate for the circumstances you'll be confronting.

Take lessons into consideration: Take lessons from competent instructors if you're brand-new to kiteboarding or surfing to master the fundamentals and crucial safety procedures.

Yachting and Sailboarding

Yacht charter: If you don't have your boat, you can rent one in Tahiti with no problem. With a variety of sailboats, catamarans, and motor yachts available for hire, the area is home to many charter businesses.

Depending on your tastes and degree of expertise, you may choose the vessel. Booking in advance is advised, particularly during the busiest travel times.

There are several well-liked sailing routes in Tahiti, each of which offers distinct experiences. Known as the "Society Islands Loop," this route is the most popular.

Tahiti, Moorea, Bora Bora, Huahine, Raiatea, and Taha'a are often included. By taking this route, you may enjoy spectacular coral reefs, iconic overwater bungalows, and the lively Polynesian culture.

Navigation and weather: Tahiti has year-round temperate temperatures and reliable trade winds, which provide for usually pleasant sailing conditions. Nevertheless, it's critical to be aware of local weather patterns and navigational obstacles like coral reefs and shallow waters.

You may either hire a local skipper to help you if you have some basic sailing and navigational ability or you can.

Tahiti offers a wide variety of mooring and anchoring locations. Numerous atolls and islands have designated areas where you can moor your boat or anchor it. Additionally, some areas have marinas and yacht clubs that offer services for upkeep as well as amenities like water, fuel, and supplies.

Activities & Attractions: While sailing in Tahiti, you may take part in several activities including snorkeling, diving, fishing, and visiting deserted islands.

In Taha'a, you can explore the coral gardens, swim with manta rays in Bora Bora, or just unwind on the white sands and clear waters.

Local customs and laws: Before setting sail for Tahiti, it is crucial to get acquainted with the laws and traditions of the region. Verify you have all the essential documentation, including a sailing license if applicable, as well as the relevant permits.

Be mindful of the ocean environment and follow rules for conserving marine life and coral reefs.

Seasonality: From May to October, the dry season, which is the greatest time for sailing and yachting in Tahiti, is when you should go.

In addition to the trade winds being stronger, the weather is more consistent at this time. Tahiti's climate, with temperatures ranging from 70°F to

90°F (21°C to 32°C), is, nonetheless, noteworthy since it is moderate and pleasant all year round.

Aquaplaning and Jet Skiing

Jet skiing is an exhilarating way to explore the nearby waterways and take in the island's stunning scenery in Tahiti.

There are several rental companies offering jet ski rentals in well-known resorts and tourist destinations.

For your safety and to show you the greatest places to visit, these companies often provide guided excursions.

You may surf the waves, zip through the emerald lagoons, find undiscovered coves, and explore beautiful beaches on a jet ski.

You may feel the rush of speed while taking in Tahiti's gorgeous surroundings during this adrenaline-pumping activity. Several jet ski trips also include breaks for swimming or snorkeling in the pristine seas.

Parasailing: Tahiti's gorgeous coastline may be seen from a whole new angle, and the surrounding Pacific Ocean can be seen from a great distance. Being pulled by a boat while being raised into the air while attached to a parachute is part of this sport.

In well-known tourist destinations or resorts along the coast, you can find parasailing providers. To guarantee your safety while participating in the activity, they normally provide the required gear and knowledgeable guides.

You'll get a birds-eye perspective of Tahiti's stunning environment as you fly above the ocean, taking in its blue lagoons, verdant mountains, and stunning vegetation.

It's not necessary to have any previous knowledge or abilities to participate in this rather easy sport. The experience is unforgettable and thrilling for individuals of all ages, especially young children.

It's crucial to wear the proper safety gear and adhere to the safety recommendations given by the operators while partaking in jet skiing and parasailing sports. To guarantee a secure and comfortable trip, also be careful of the regional laws and regulations.

Visits with Dolphins and Whale Watching

Whale watching and dolphin interactions may be had in awe-inspiring surroundings in Tahiti, which is in French Polynesia.

The area is a popular travel destination for those who like the outdoors and animals because of the area's temperate seas, which are home to many different kinds of whales and dolphins.

Here is some information to aid you in organizing your whale-watching and dolphin encounters in Tahiti, while exact experiences may vary depending on the season and regional conditions:

Whale viewing in Tahiti is most popular from July to November. This is the best time to go. For breeding and nursing purposes, humpback whales travel at this time to the hospitable seas of French Polynesia.

This is the season when you have a better chance of seeing these magnificent animals.

Guided whale viewing trips are provided by several travel companies in Tahiti. Papeete (the nation's capital), Moorea, or Bora Bora are a few of the common starting points for these excursions.

They are escorted by qualified guides who have firsthand knowledge of the behavior and features of the whales and utilize boats suitable for observing marine animals. To guarantee a position on the trip, it's a good idea to make a reservation in advance.

Though dolphin sightings are possible all year long in Tahiti, some regions are more likely to experience them than others. Particularly well-known for its dolphin populations is Moorea, an island close to Tahiti.

There, you may often see spinner and bottlenose dolphins. A few travel companies provide escorted tours that let you swim and interact with these amusing animals in their natural environment. To protect the dolphins' welfare, these interactions are often undertaken under rigorous regulations.

Select tour companies that place a priority on responsible and ethical practices when participating in whale watching or dolphin encounters. To reduce disruptions to wildlife and their habitats, look for operators that adhere to rules and laws. The well-being of the animals and the preservation of their natural habits depend on respectful conduct, which includes keeping a safe distance from the wildlife, minimizing noise, and refraining from touching or feeding the animals.

Keep in mind that seeing wildlife is never certain since it depends on a variety of things, including the weather and the animals' normal habits.

The breathtaking scenery and rich marine life of Tahiti, however, provide a fantastic opportunity to see these wonderful animals up close and in their native habitat. Take in the sights of the water and your adventure.

Adventures Off-Road on the Island

Exploring the natural splendor and varied landscapes of this idyllic island paradise is made possible by off-road excursions through Tahiti. Tahiti has plenty to offer everyone, whether they are thrill-seekers searching for exhilarating rides or nature lovers wishing to get lost in the island's unspoiled environment.

Safari Jeep Tours: Embark on a guided jeep excursion that ventures far into Tahiti's lush valleys, craggy mountains, and sparkling waterfalls. These excursions provide a unique blend of action, cultural knowledge, and stunning landscape.

Get on an all-terrain quad bike and ride through rocky landscapes, muddy trails, and dense forests. Off-road roads, beautiful vistas, and undiscovered treasures in Tahiti's wilderness may all be explored at your leisure.

Book a 4x4 adventure to discover the island's many topographies, such as its volcanic peaks, black sand beaches, and tropical rainforests.

Your knowledgeable guides will take you through off-road routes while telling you tales about Tahiti's history, flora, and animals.

Mountain bike: Take on a new challenge when mountain biking in Tahiti. Experience the exhilaration of biking across rocky paths and down steep descents while seeing the island's natural treasures. There are possibilities for bikers of all ability levels, from seaside excursions to interior paths.

Waterfall Hiking: Combine hiking and off-roading to explore Tahiti's magnificent waterfalls. Reach hidden cascades tucked away in the center of the island by hiking through lush vegetation, crossing rivers, and crossing terrain.

If you want to cool yourself in the pristine waters, don't forget your swimwear.

Embark on a horseback riding excursion through Tahiti's beautiful landscapes by mounting up. To connect with nature, see panoramic vistas, and learn about the island's distinctive flora and wildlife, follow knowledgeable guides as they take you through off-road routes.

Tours by Helicopter: If you want a more opulent off-road adventure, think about taking a tour by helicopter. Take in the island's untamed beauty as you soar above it and take in the breath-taking aerial views of its dramatic coasts, angular mountains, and turquoise lagoons.

A chance to fly into isolated locations for a closer look is also provided by certain trips.

Embark on an exhilarating off-road adventure across Tahiti's sandy landscapes with a dune buggy excursion. Drive across scenic beaches and coastal dunes while experiencing an adrenaline rush on difficult off-road courses.

Off-Road Waterfall Rappelling: Try waterfall rappelling to elevate your off-road excursion to new heights. Off-road hiking may be combined with the thrilling experience of tumbling down cascading waterfalls using ropes and harnesses.

A thrilling approach to appreciate the island's natural splendor is via this exclusive activity.

Join a tour that explores a cave to delve into the dark recesses of Tahiti's underground world. Discover the island's geological wonders as you explore intricate cave networks and stunning stalactite formations.

Canyoning: Enjoy the rush of canyoning while navigating Tahiti's canyons, rappelling down waterfalls, navigating purely natural rock slides, and swimming in crystal-clear pools.

This thrilling activity mixes obstacles on the water with off-road trekking for an exciting experience.

UTV Adventures: Take on Tahiti's challenging terrain in a UTV (Utility Task Vehicle) to indulge your spirit of adventure.

These adaptable off-road vehicles provide you the opportunity to explore the island at your own leisure, getting to distant locations and having the freedom to find secret places.

Nature Walks & Bird Watching: For an off-road experience that is more tranquil, choose a nature walk or a bird-watching tour. These activities provide visitors to Tahiti the chance to examine the diverse range of plants, animals, and bird species that live there.

Off-Road Camping: Continue your off-road experience by pitching a tent in Tahiti's wilderness. Immerse yourself in the peace of nature by setting a tent in designated areas.

Enjoy the outdoors, make lifelong memories beneath the starry sky, and wake up to breathtaking vistas.

Never forget to ask local tour guides about each activity's availability, safety precautions, and any other prerequisites. While having fun on your Tahiti off-road excursions, always put your safety and the protection of the island's environment first.

Sailing Expeditions to the Islands

Incredibly exciting sailing excursions are available in Tahiti, a French Polynesian island nation. Tahiti is a haven for explorers and sailors with its emerald seas, luxuriant greenery, and rich Polynesian culture. When sailing in Tahiti, check out some of these well-known islands:

Tahiti is made up of two major islands: Tahiti Nui, which is the bigger of the two, and Tahiti Iti, which is the smaller. Tahiti Nui is where you should start your exploration of Tahiti.

Experience the bustling markets, energetic atmosphere, and French Polynesian cuisine of the capital, Papeete.

The island of Moorea, which is just a short sail from Tahiti, is renowned for its stunning mountain peaks, immaculate beaches, and bright coral reefs. Discover the lush valleys of the island, hike to the tops of the mountains, and go diving or snorkeling in the clear lagoons.

Bora Bora: Frequently ranked among the most stunning islands in the world, Bora Bora is a must-see location. Its recognizable turquoise lagoon, overwater bungalows, and majestous Mount Otemanu combine to create a beautiful scene.

Take advantage of the rich aquatic life by swimming, snorkeling, or diving.

Raiatea, sometimes referred to as the "Sacred Island," is regarded as the cultural and historical center of French Polynesia. Learn about Polynesian history and navigation while exploring its beautiful landscapes and historic marae (sacred places). Sailing charters in the region sometimes leave from Raiatea as well.

Huahine: This undiscovered island is a jewel that provides a more relaxed and genuine experience. Ancient archaeological ruins, coral gardens, and lovely beaches may all be found on Huahine.

Explore the quaint villages on the island, get to know the people there, and become familiar with Polynesian customs.

Taha'a: Frequently called the "Vanilla Island," Taha'a is well-known for its vanilla plantations and enticing aromas. Visit a vanilla plantation, wander through the verdant valleys of the island, and unwind on the isolated beaches. Together with its neighbor Raiatea, Taha'a also has a stunning lagoon that is ideal for sailing and snorkeling.

Tetiaroa: A private atoll with an interesting history and stunning natural beauty, Tetiaroa is a little remote from the other islands. It was subsequently owned by Marlon Brando.

It was formerly the private hideaway of Tahitian nobility. Investigate the atoll's immaculate beaches, vibrant coral reefs, and variety of bird species.

If you want to sail independently or with a crew, decide this before you start your sailing adventure. Tahiti's many tour firms and charter businesses provide sailing programs to fit a range of tastes and price ranges.

For your sailing trip, make sure you have the required licenses, navigational skills, and safety gear.

Respect the native culture, the maritime environment, and the protected regions. Tahiti is the perfect location for a sailing vacation you'll never forget since its islands provide many options for exploration, adventure, and relaxation.

CONCLUSION

A sensation of peace overcame me as I walked onto Tahiti's gorgeous coastline. The blue seas shimmered in the warmth of the sun, and the air was filled with the soft rustling of palm palms. I had really visited Tahiti, the idyllic island I had always imagined.

During my visit, I fully immersed myself in the vibrant Polynesian culture. I wandered through the busy marketplaces, admiring the proud stalls where residents proudly showed their homemade wares.

As I admired the artistry and craftsmanship all around me, the vivid colors of the pareos and flower crowns engulfed my senses.

New experiences awaited you every day. Following the sound of tumbling waterfalls that took me to undiscovered treasures, I set out on an exhilarating journey through deep jungles.

I was in awe of the island's beautiful surroundings and couldn't help but feel a strong connection to nature because of their pure beauty.

The locals of Tahiti greeted me with open arms and warm grins that captured the essence of the islands. I was filled with excitement as I danced to the beat of the traditional Tahitian drums.

I was engulfed in the community's contagious happiness and gained a renewed enthusiasm for life.

I took comfort in the serenity of the nights as the sun fell below the horizon. The starlit evenings have a calming backdrop supplied by the lapping of the waves on the coast.

I took a leisurely walk down the sand, feeling the smooth sand between my toes, while admiring the vastness of the night sky and the stars that gleamed with an unmatched brightness there.

I learned the genuine meaning of mindfulness and present-moment acceptance in Tahiti. I took my time enjoying each dawn, letting the colors paint the sky with their magnificent colours.

Fresh tropical fruits were delicious, and their sweetness reminded me of the abundance of nature's gifts. And I loved being with my new pals; their tales and laughter resonated in my heart.

As my time in Tahiti came to an end, I was thankful for the experiences that had changed me. My soul had been reawakened by the island, and I now felt a burning desire to experience life to the utmost. Tahiti's spirit was woven into the fabric of my being and was permanently inscribed in my memory.

Tahiti had provided me with more than just a brief reprieve. It had given me a great insight of the interdependence of all things as well as a deep appreciation of the world's beauty.

I learned through it that paradise is a state of mind and a way of seeing the world with awe and thankfulness, not simply a physical location.

I had a tear in my eye as I said goodbye to Tahiti, but it was a pleasure. I understood that this magical island had merged with me and that its soul would always direct my travels. I departed to discover new horizons with a heart overflowing with appreciation and a newfound zeal for life.

I carried the enchantment of Tahiti in my spirit and yearned for the day when I would return to the embrace of its beauty.

Printed in Great Britain
by Amazon